The TIFFANY WEDDING

John Loring

Introduction by Patricia Warner
Location Photography by Peter Vitale

Doubleday
NEW YORK LONDON TORONTO SYDNEY

Also by John Loring:
TIFFANY'S 150 YEARS
TIFFANY TASTE
THE NEW TIFFANY TABLE
SETTINGS (with Henry B. Platt)

Designed by Jean-Claude Suarès

Published by Doubleday, a division of
Bantam Doubleday Dell Publishing
Group, Inc., 666 Fifth Avenue,
New York, New York 10103.

Doubleday and the portrayal of an
anchor with a dolphin are trademarks of
Doubleday, a division of Bantam
Doubleday Dell Publishing Group, Inc.

Library of Congress Cataloging-in-
Publication Data
Loring, John.
  The Tiffany wedding.
  1. Weddings.   I. Title.
BJ2051.L85   1988   395'.22   87-36414

ISBN 0-385-24101-1

Acknowledgments
· · · · · · · ·

Tiffany & Co. gratefully acknowledges
the exceptional contributions of Yone
Akiyama, Tiffany's Associate Design Director, for her role as director of photography; Eleanor Lambert (Berkson)
for her selection and coordination of
fashions; Mr. John Cherol of The Pres-
ervation Society of Newport County for
his assistance with Newport locations;
Ms. Sheila Donnelly for her assistance
with Hawaii locations; and Mr. John
Innes for his expertise in fashion styling.

pages 2–3

*U*nder the shade of hackberry and
pecan trees on the Duncanville,
Texas, ranch of Mr. and Mrs.
J. W. Pinkerton, the bride's and
groom's families join in a country
engagement-party dinner. The down-
home style is full of charm. Tables
are covered with an heirloom quilt
and counterpane, and barrels and
bales of hay serve as extra side tables and for seating.

The Pinkertons' prizewinning cutting horses, Son of Real Doe, Cal's
Cutter, Brinks Hickory Ann, and
Goodbye Lisa, stay as close to the
celebration as possible.

Dinner will finish with an imaginative chocolate "Texas oil well
cake" by Dallas-based Paul Jerabek
of Special Affairs Catering.

The rifles are added for local color,
not in anticipation of a "shotgun"
wedding.

frontispiece

*I*n studied understatement, the mil-
lionaires of America's Gilded Age
called their Newport summer palaces
"cottages." Of all Newport's cottages,
The Breakers, built for Cornelius
Vanderbilt by Richard Hunt, is unquestionably the grandest.

The Vanderbilts' housewarming,
combined with the coming-out party
of their twenty-year-old daughter
Gertrude, was held at The Breakers
one August evening in 1895. A year
later on August 25, 1896, in the
Music Room, Gertrude Vanderbilt
married Harry Payne Whitney wearing this sumptuous heavy-satin
bridal gown.

Mrs. Whitney's dress is pictured
in her bedroom where she dressed for
the wedding.

Her portrait by Helleu hangs over
her dresser, which holds family photos, the garland of artificial orange
blossoms she wore as a bridal coiffe,
and a bronze figure she sculpted in
later life.

Gertrude Vanderbilt Whitney went
on to found the Whitney Museum of
American Art.

facing page

*P*ew bows designed by Boston florist
Tom Rogers for the Federal-style
chapel of Middlesex School outside
Concord, Massachusetts, are composed of casablanca lilies, white sweet
peas, asparagus fern, and Swedish
ruscus leaves, all tied with multiple
pink satin ribbons.

Contents

· · · · · · · ·

THE *TIFFANY WEDDING* OFFERS A SINGLE suggestion: make the most of the best moments of life.

What may seem like a labyrinth of social form and convention surrounding the wedding is only there to give structure and guidance to the overall celebration and to provide limitless opportunity for spirited enjoyment.

No other occasion is lavished with as much attention and detailing as the wedding. Yet, the intricacy of the proceedings should not inhibit the imagination.

After all the planning, script writing, casting, producing, and rehearsing is done, the performance should have style, beauty, and charm. Surrounding its moving central moments there should be a sense of great good fun.

It is a celebration, and *The Tiffany Wedding* says, "Celebrate!"

Weddings may be gala or simple, large or small, but each and every one should, in its own way, be extravagant, imaginative, and unique.

The Tiffany Wedding is an idealized portrait of the American wedding from Tiffany's perspective. After 150 years of supplying Americans with the invitations, the rings, the china, crystal, and silver,

and the attendants' gifts for American weddings both great and small, Tiffany's has acquired a panoramic vision of the stylistic diversity that America offers.

Regional atmosphere and custom play a larger role than one might at first suspect. To illustrate the variety of possibilities for every detail of American weddings, Tiffany's presents a photographic journey across the United States; from Newport's palace-lined Bellevue Avenue to the wine-growing valleys of central California; from the colonial plantations of Virginia's James River to the imperial villas of Dallas and Fort Worth; from a Park Avenue maisonette to a planter's cottage on a Hawaiian lagoon, with a stopover on a movie star's sailing yacht in San Francisco Bay.

The expertise and authority of leading American fashion designers, editors, hostesses, caterers, florists, party designers, bakers, restaurateurs, and hotelkeepers have been joined with Tiffany's own expertise to create this portrait of the wedding, with all-American vigor, stylishness, and invention.

John Loring

facing page

Mrs. Charles Scribner, Jr., and her bridal party.

left

Mrs. Post, the daughter of Mr. and Mrs. Charles Dana Gibson, was married to Mr. George B. Post, Jr., son of Mr. and Mrs. George B. Post, at St. Bartholomew's Church. It was one of the brilliant weddings of the season with all smart society in attendance and most of the best-known artists and literary people of New York.

THE ENGAGEMENT

OU'RE ENGAGED! THE STARRY-EYED announcement to family and friends is greeted with a mixture of pleasure, nostalgia, and hope. The future is an imagined adventure based on emotions, and on dreams as old as time.

From the moment two people make their declaration, they become a future bride and groom. The mood is euphoric; feelings run high; and it is time to make a strategic plan.

Expertise, in tandem with custom and common sense, will serve to lighten the awesomeness of it all. Planning a wedding, especially a large, traditional wedding, is like movie making. It needs a script; it needs a budget; it needs a director. All it has from the start is a cast. Someone must bring in the extras, the location, props, and costumes, so that when the final cut is made it is an award-winning production. This is the moment to decide whether to hire a wedding consultant to oversee the entire day, or a party planner to mastermind the reception only, or both.

A consultant can guide you through thorny matters of etiquette, settle family disputes with impartiality, and offer creative solutions. Consultants locate the best in limousine services, caterers, bakers, musicians, and florists. Their familiarity with other professionals can do much to defray costs and keep things on course. Ms. Barbara Feldman, popular Westchester bridal consultant in the business for twenty-one years, wisely counsels: "Time is important. Allow enough of it. A week before a wedding, check every supplier involved. No matter how small the detail—check it. Run through an at-home reception to see that coatracks are in place, soap and hand towels are in the

bathrooms. I always recommend valet parking, so that the caterers' or musicians' vans don't accidentally block the guests' cars, for example."

If the wedding is to be a small, private ceremony with a big, splashy reception, a party planner may be the right choice. They deal with renting tents and equipment, where necessary; with the catering, the decorations, and the entertainment, as well as with the all-important question of styling the wedding to suit your vision. The best consultants or planners are frequently found by word of mouth, but bridal magazines are also an excellent resource. Settle the method of payment for their services beforehand, and be sure there is a letter of agreement between you. If you choose to choreograph the occasion yourselves, read on.

In any family, extended or otherwise, the wedding plans will take over and normal life will take second place. As it is with any stage mother, so it is with the mother of the bride. She is a force of nature. Some young brides are glad to concede everything to that ball of energy, and most brides will recognize her usefulness. Who better to stand up to an overbearing stylist who wants to deck the reception with pink tulle swags when you want evergreens? Or light a fire under the helpers when things get tardy? Involve your mother in decisions regarding location, catering, and decoration, especially if she and her husband are footing the wedding reception bill. Outings to the dressmaker and trousseau shopping accompanied by her, even if your tastes differ, will be invaluable. And she is going to air her views anyway.

Your future husband's "talk with Father" is nearly obsolete. Nowadays, couples with individual assets to consider settle their affairs with a premarital agreement, which is explained in more detail on page 43. However, whether you are upwardly mobile or just rich, your parents will appreciate your concern with money matters. So, have a cards-on-the-table discussion with them, together with your groom, and assuage any fears about your future. If the respective parents are not acquainted, they will wish to arrange a get-together; your marriage is an undertaking for them as well.

The most sensitive of all situations is the presence of children from a previous marriage. Assuming the child has already met his or her potential stepparent and formed a friendship, talk your plans over with him or her as soon as possible and notice the reaction. Stepchildren's genuine liking for the new person in their life can lead to a confusion of allegiances in their minds. Problems such as these require cosmic dimensions of patience and understanding. Premarital counseling, helpful in any case, is most beneficial here.

THE ENGAGEMENT RING

The Diamond

The jewel that glitters on your finger tells the world of a promise made. Since the fifteenth century, the tender pledges of kings and nobles have been sealed with a diamond. The diamond is prized as a bridal jewel: radiant on a gold band, either solitaire or set between side stones. Its purity represents the innocence of the bride-to-be; its immutability the strength of the commitment. Because of their clear, hard, brilliant transparency, gems were considered miraculous, mystical; the touchstones to the spirit and even the conductor of men's thoughts. Placing the ring on the third finger of the left hand was done on the assumption that a vein ran from this finger directly to the heart, a notion the ancient Romans took from the Egyptians. The Elizabethans, in their contrary way, would often as not wear their pledge ring on their thumb.

The fame of the diamond surpasses that of any other stone. A rare, flawless specimen of extraordinary carat weight and size can inspire awe some feel before a great work of art. Ancient superstitions have attributed remarkable talismanic powers to gems. The diamond was believed to confer courage upon the wearer, and protection from evil and disease. Until the eighteenth century, diamonds were used in medicine—pulverized and swallowed in drafts.

Gem cutting was developed in France and the Netherlands in the early fifteenth century. As pure or nearly pure carbon, a diamond is of course the hardest substance on earth. It was discovered that

Gilt wood and marble rococo cherubs hold candles and rubrum lilies in this ornament, which adds to the abundant romanticism at an outdoor dinner after the wedding reception.

THE TIFFANY WEDDING

13

cutting and polishing released the mineral's unique qualities of light refraction. India is the oldest source for diamonds, a treasure trove that once supplied the princely courts of Asia and Europe with magnificent specimens. Today the majority of diamonds come from South Africa, where the first stone was discovered in 1867. In the classic solitaire the stone is "brilliant" cut, with fifty-eight triangular facets that act as prisms. The resulting cone shape is held away from the band within a six-prong setting for optimum interplay between the diamond and light.

There is no doubting the views of Tiffany's senior gemologist, Peter Schneirla, upon the engagement ring: "We take a position on the matter of the diamond solitaire. It is the right symbol for the occasion and, because of its meaning, will become the most unique item in the woman's jewelry wardrobe."

Buying a diamond, or any fine gemstone, can be spellbinding and quite unlike any other experience. The factors that determine the quality of a diamond are popularly known as the four C's: clarity, color, carat, and cut.

Clarity refers to the absence of flaws, although a truly flawless diamond is extremely rare. Color means the "whiter" the stone, the greater its value. Diamonds can be yellow, brown, pink, green, or blue. Carat is the standard for measuring the actual weight of the stone. One one-hundredth of a carat is called a point, so a one-quarter-carat diamond may be also expressed decimally as a .25-point stone. Cut is the slicing and faceting of the rough stone to ideal, mathematically calculated proportions. Light will ignite a diamond's fire and beauty. A well-cut diamond will return light to the eye in the form of brilliance; make it sparkle, which is called scintillation, and break it up into a spectrum of colors, referred to as dispersion.

A 2-carat diamond has the same diameter, more or less, as a garden pea. Schneirla, commenting on the relationship of size and cut, says, "Once you get close to ten carats, round diamonds tend to resemble headlights. The rough of bigger diamonds lend themselves to emerald cut or fancy shapes. Pear or heart-shaped is the second most sought-after form for an engagement ring." Further explaining the mystique of jewels, he says, "There is a sharp line between diamonds and other gemstones. Cutting a diamond demands waste to bring the colored lights to it, and the process is strictly controlled. Other stones may be cut in any fashion; the color is intrinsic." Historic diamond shapes, besides the "brilliant cut" thought to have been invented in Venice around 1700, are the seventeenth-century Dutch and Antwerp rose cuts, the pear, oval, emerald, marquise, and heart shapes.

The Sapphire

There are those who believe, along with British royalty, that an engagement ring should include a peerless sapphire, token of faithfulness and heavenly bliss. Sapphires and rubies derive from the gem mineral corundum. As translucent stones, they are cut with facets to preserve the depth of color, and are perfect as ring stones.

Sapphires exist in many colors besides blue: pale pink, yellow, green, violet, gray, and colorless. There is no red sapphire; a red corundum is a ruby. A superb blue sapphire is a deep cornflower blue, exhibiting a faint silvery sheen known as "silk." American sapphires from Montana are characteristically small, but bright with color. Because of their mineral composition, sapphires will alter color in different lights. Kashmir sapphires, historically the finest, are rare. Other sources, besides America, are Cambodia, Thailand, and Sri Lanka, which was called the "Isle of Gems" by the Chinese. Australia produces dark blue, blue-green, and yellow sapphires.

The Ruby

The ruby and emerald are the most valuable gemstones on earth. Rubies have long inspired fantasy and superstition. The Hindus associated the ruby with fire and imagined that it radiated heat. Rubies were supposed to quell nightmares, cure ailments, and ensure love, peace, and happiness. For centuries, fabulous rubies have been mined in the Mogok district of Upper Burma; most notably the extraordinary Burmese stones called "pigeon's-blood"—now as rare as hen's teeth.

A fine ruby is an intense red and, like the sapphire, is second only to the diamond as the hardest mineral substance. The ruby's fiery beauty and prestige prompted Britain's Prince Andrew to break a royal custom when he became engaged to Lady Sarah Ferguson. He chose a fine oval ruby ring, with ten drop (pear-shaped) diamonds set cluster style, perhaps in tribute to her flowing titian hair.

The Emerald

The emerald's ancient connection with the goddess Venus makes it another compelling choice for an engagement ring. But note, it was also thought that should the man and woman's relationship go awry, the emerald would immediately shatter.

Most emeralds are cut in a rectangular fashion because of the nature of the original crystal. A skilled cutter will waste less material while enhancing the emerald's magical green, which should be deep without a hint of yellow or blue. For centuries, the most sought-after stones have originated in Colombia and Brazil. Other sources are the Far East, Africa and, lately, Pakistan.

The Guest List

The guest list, as everyone soon discovers, can expand to the unmanageable. The diplomatic method is to apportion one third for each of the two families, the remainder for friends of the bride and groom. The trouble begins when one family has more members, or more close friends. Also, the family that is paying the bills may expect a bigger voice. While keeping matters of protocol in mind, remember it is *your* wedding. When every person to whom the wedding is important has been counted and you have sidestepped inviting those remote third cousins from Milwaukee, let affection, humor, and tact be your guide.

STATIONERY

Invitations

Formal or informal, the invitation will provide a clue to your wedding's style. A formal invitation is engraved, usually in black ink in traditional script on heavy white or cream-colored paper, either folded or as a single sheet. An informal invitation might have a modern typeface, printed in green ink on a pale blue card or blue ink on a white card; the choice is endless. Thermographic printing, because it mimics engraving, is a popular and less expensive substitute for either formally or informally worded invitations. The ink is mixed with powder, which produces a raised lettering that tends to shine as if it has been polished.

Within extended families, or for interfaith marriages, wording of invitations can become complex. Reputable stationers have a staff trained to help. There are erroneous ways to issue an invitation, no matter how informal, so put your trust in an expert.

Dr. and Mrs. Thomas Allen Greene

BELGRAVE SCRIPT

Mr. and Mrs. Richard Arthur Hyman

HAMILTON

Mr. and Mrs. Richard Murray Barton

LIGHT SCRIPT

The standard form, if the invitation is from the bride's parents, will read:

Mr. and Mrs. John James Smith, Jr.

request the honour of your presence

at the marriage of their daughter

Mary Elizabeth

to

Mr. Peter Edward Jones

Saturday, the twenty-fifth of June

at four o'clock

Saint Andrew's Church

Lawrenceville, New Jersey

If the wedding is being given jointly with the groom's parents, their name should appear on the invitation as well, after the bride's parents. The date, time, and address are always spelled out.

The reception invitation may be combined by adding:

And afterwards at

Five Ten Heavenly Lodge, Wicker's Lane

R.S.V.P.

A separate reception invitation card will read:

Reception

immediately following the ceremony

Jarvis Court Country Club

Fourteen Syosset Road

Long Island, New York

R.S.V.P.

Mr. and Mrs. Percival Harold Clayton

MAYFAIR

Mr and Mrs John Low Venable

LONDON SCRIPT

Mr. and Mrs. Hugh Robert Scott

PARSIFAL

Your guests should reply with a telephone call or note in good time for you to plan the numbers for the reception.

Invitations to a Roman Catholic wedding may say, after the couple's names: "will be united in the Sacrament of Marriage." A divorced couple conducting their own second marriage may say:

The honour of your presence

is requested at the marriage of

Sarah Jane Barton

to

George Soames Winston

The minimum order is usually one hundred invitations, and includes two matching envelopes. The larger, outer envelope may be engraved or embossed with the return address on either the envelope flap or upper left front. The inner envelope, always sent unsealed, holds the invitation.

Enclosures embrace the several other steps you will wish to consider. A separate reception card, already mentioned above, allows you to invite some people to the church ceremony only; an at-home card, which indicates the post-honeymoon arrival date and married address of the newlyweds, is optional.

Allow four to six weeks for delivery after ordering the invitations. The printer or stationer will help by sending the outer envelopes ahead to be addressed, if you request it. Envelopes must be handwritten, with the full name and address, including zip code, of the recipients. Invitations should be sent to each of the attendants and, if feasible, their parents. Adult children eighteen years and older from either family should receive their own invitation. The regular companion of a single guest should be invited as well, but you do not have to provide blind dates for other singles. Invitations to unmarried couples, or couples where the woman has kept her maiden name, should be addressed with both names on separate lines in either alphabetical order or with the woman's name first.

Mr. and Mrs. Anthony Ross Hagen

Dr. and Mrs. Jay Barclay Woods

Reverend and Mrs. William Carlsen

SAINT JAMES

TALLEYRAND

WINDSOR

When the full invitation order is delivered, again write in ink the name of your guests on the inner envelopes, using: Mr. and Mrs. Jones, or Ms. Brown, and omitting first names. Mail the invitations six to eight weeks prior to the wedding.

Coordinate the graphic elements at your wedding by ordering your place cards, menu cards, and fold-over match covers in the same style as your invitations. Plan this ahead with your stationer, so that you can place the order quickly when all the acceptances are in hand. Place your order for your personal stationery at this time, to be monogrammed with your married initials.

Announcements

Publish the announcement of your engagement in your local newspaper for the wider world to appreciate, by contacting the society editor one or two weeks before you wish the news to appear. The editor will convey to you the proper form for the wording of an engagement or a marriage announcement.

Submit a formal portrait, by a professional photographer, in the form of an 8 by 10-inch black-and-white print. A wedding head and shoulder portrait of the bride must be taken in good time to send a print to the newspaper, so that it can run with your marriage notice. The editor will request this about ten days before publication (generally the day after or the first Sunday after the wedding). If your fiancé is to be included, he too should be wearing his wedding finery.

The engagement of Mary Elizabeth Smith to Peter Edward Jones has been announced by Mr. and Mrs. John James Smith, Jr., of Lawrenceville, New Jersey, parents of the future bride. Her fiancé is the son of Mr. and Mrs. George B. Jones of Cambridge, Massachusetts. A June wedding is planned.

Ms. Smith is a graphic designer. She attended the Princeton Day School, and was graduated from Barnard College in 1987. Her father is a vice president of the Chase

MR. AND MRS. SPENCER WOODS MILLER

LEHMAN ROMAN

Mr. and Mrs. Robert William Sloane

SPAULDING CLASSIC

Mr. and Mrs. Daniel Montgomery, Jr.

SHADED ANTIQUE ROMAN

Manhattan Bank. The bride-to-be is the granddaughter of Arthur Hughes of New York, who was a partner in the brokerage firm of Smith Barney, and Mrs. Hughes, and the late Mr. and Mrs. Richard Smith.

Mr. Jones, a graduate of New York University, expects to receive a Master of Business Administration from Columbia University in May of next year. His father is director of scientific affairs at Creekmore Laboratories in Boston. His mother is a professor of history at Harvard University.

Mary Elizabeth Smith, daughter of Mr. and Mrs. John James Smith, Jr., of Lawrenceville, New Jersey, was married there yesterday to Peter Edward Jones. He is the son of Mr. and Mrs. George B. Jones of Cambridge, Mass. The Rev. William Watson performed the ceremony at St. Andrew's Church.

Judith Schwartz was the maid of honor. The bridesmaids were Lucy Ann Tuckerman and Priscilla Smith, sisters of the bride, and Jennifer J. Watson, sister of the bridegroom. Beth Middleton and Rebecca Collins, cousins of the bride, were the flower girls. Keith Simon was the best man. The ushers were Howard Dawson, Stephen Henry, Nicholas Barrett, and Matthew Cohen.

The bride, a graphic designer, attended the Princeton Day School and was graduated from Barnard College in 1987. Her father is a vice president of the Chase Manhattan Bank. Mrs. Jones is the granddaughter of Arthur Hughes of New York, who was a partner in the brokerage firm of Smith Barney, and Mrs. Hughes, and the late Mr. and Mrs. Richard Smith.

Mr. Jones, a graduate of New York University, expects to receive a Master of Business Administration from Columbia University next May. His father is director of scientific affairs at Creekmore Laboratories in Boston. His mother is a professor of history at Harvard University.

Custom has provided the bride-to-be with many more formal prewedding entertainments than will be enjoyed by her fiancé. To help redress this seeming inequity, Tiffany's proposes a setting for "His Last Dinner Alone" designed by New York artist Richard Taddei.

The groom's table is set with "Hampton" flat silver, Wedgwood basalt ware, and "Eva" crystal stemware. A Tiffany silver frame holds the photo of a favorite pet, who will be receiving less attention after the wedding. The scene is backed by Richard Taddei's painting Raining Cats and Chairs.

THE ENGAGEMENT PARTY

Few fathers would pass up their moments of glory as the father of the bride. The official engagement party, customarily given by the bride's parents, allows him his first opportunity to play the rough but loving patriarch, ruefully committing his precious girl to another's keeping. Of course, a friend can give you your engagement party if your parents are unable to.

The engagement party should have a relaxed, welcoming informality: a cocktail party, buffet supper, even a garden barbecue are all ideal. Sending printed or engraved invitations is a good idea, since many guests may not know one another, yet find they have the same happy event to celebrate. The wording for an engraved invitation from the parents should read:

> We request the pleasure of your company at a
> cocktail [or whatever] party, in celebration
> of the engagement of
> our daughter,
> Mary Ann
> to
> John William Greeves
> at [day, time, and location]

Or if the engagement announcement is to be a surprise, the hosts may simply invite everyone to a party.

At an opportune moment in the festivities, the bride's father announces the glad news and proposes a toast to the couple. Your fiancé can respond with words of thanks, to which his father will want to add his acknowledgments and appreciation. No one is expected to bring engagement presents, since everyone gathered should also be invited to the wedding. The engagement party is the bride's big moment to display the splendid engagement ring now adorning her finger—officially the first time she wears it. It is at this event, or very soon after, that the father gives his daughter her personal bridal gift from him.

CHOOSING THE ATTENDANTS

The engagement party is over, the wedding date set, and the days of tumult about to begin. It is the

This page, lovingly painted and colored by Olive Bigelow Pell in 1929 in the family album of Rhode Island's Pells, exemplifies with great charm the solemnity and celebration that mark the American wedding.

moment to invite close relatives and favorite friends to be your attendants; to fill time-honored supportive roles and, with their decorative presence, complete the wedding-day tableau.

For the Bride

Brides choose bridesmaids contemporary in age to themselves, as a rule. Once upon a time, unmarried "maids" assumed the honor, but this is too tribal an idea for today's tastes: married and pregnant women may now participate. The bride needs an attendant even at the smallest wedding. The full-blown spectacular can involve eight or more bridesmaids, junior bridesmaids, flower girls, a ring bearer, two or more pages, a maid and a matron of honor. The flower girl is the sprite, between the ages of four and eight, who will trip the aisle carrying a basketful of flowers, paper rose petals, or rice packets, to be handed out later. The ring bearer, a boy or girl aged between three and seven, holds a small cushion with a plain, inexpensive ring firmly stitched in place, symbolic of the wedding rings themselves. Pages are little boys who carry the bride's train, and melt everyone's heart. A junior bridesmaid, aged between nine and sixteen, is generally an immediate relative of the bride or groom. She attends the bride, but is not expected to stand in the receiving line afterward.

Adults who accept your invitation to be bridesmaids take on certain responsibilities as members of the wedding party. They are expected to pay for their own dresses and accessories, in most cases, and to participate in prewedding events: a bridal shower; the bridesmaids' luncheon; the rehearsal, and to stand on the receiving line at the reception.

The Maid or Matron of Honor (Honor Attendant)

The maid (or matron, if married) of honor plays her role at the ceremony itself, although prior to the wedding she may help with the invitations or oversee the bridesmaids' costumes. The bride usually chooses her sister or a very dear friend—never her mother, who will be busy enough as hostess of the occasion.

A maid or matron of honor holds the bride's bouquet during the service and keeps the groom's wedding ring (if used) to pass to the officiate. It is she who will lift the bride's veil from her face at the altar, help settle her train, keep the child attendants in place, and sign the marriage license as a witness. You can have both a maid and a matron of honor to share these tasks. As your personal attendants, they are meant to help you into your wedding finery and later your going-away clothes, see that you are properly packed, and be guardian angels to you and your mother throughout the celebrations.

The Groom's Best Man

The best man is chosen by the groom and is often a brother, cousin, reliable friend, or perhaps his father or stepfather. The best man has a pivotal role in the entire proceedings, as coordinator, toastmaster, and personal aide to the groom. In the bad old days of arranged marriages, he acted frequently as the couple's messenger and the families' go-between in the financial negotiations.

The best man's initial task is to help the groom organize the bachelor dinner. He attends the rehearsal and ensures that the ushers are present. On the wedding day, he helps the groom dress and makes sure he arrives at the ceremony in good time. The best man marshals the ushers and takes charge of the bride's wedding ring, the groom's gloves, and the marriage license, which he signs as one of the witnesses.

At the reception, he sits to the right of the bride and proposes the first toast to the newlyweds. He reads aloud the congratulatory telegrams, and will go on too long if nobody stops him. It is the best man who holds for safekeeping the travel tickets and checks; who stows the luggage and makes sure that the getaway vehicle is ready to leave at the appointed time.

The Ushers

The ushers are picked by the groom from among relatives and good friends. He can have as many as he wishes; however, one usher to fifty guests is the standard equation. The usher conducts family members and guests to their places at the ceremony, offering his right arm to each lady. The groom's mother is seated before the bride's mother, who is seated last. Once she is in her place, the ceremony can begin. Ushers walk in pairs, the taller ones behind; an extra usher walks alone.

After the service and following the recessional, during which each usher escorts a bridesmaid, the ushers again conduct parents and reserved pew guests out, and remove the pew ribbons to allow the other guests to follow. Some ushers will help spirit the bridal party to the reception ahead of the rest, in order to form the receiving line. Others see guests to their transportation and safely to the reception. Then, apart from being thoroughly charming and mingling with the guests, their duties are done.

THE NEW BRIDAL REGISTRY

Bridal registries offer a comprehensive service allowing you to register your every desire, from a porcelain service for twenty-four to an exercise bike to a sterling silver birdcage.

As soon as the engagement is announced, you should register for your gifts at one or several department or specialty stores, where a personal bridal consultant will be assigned to you. Bridal gift registries are staffed by professionals with invaluable knowledge in the bridal area. Their sympathetic attention will support and guide your decisions. Your lists are computer-recorded and available at all branches of the store. Remember to list items in a wide range of prices, allowing guests to select a present that fits their budget. Word of mouth is the customary way to let friends and relatives know where you have left lists. They are relieved of indecision and can pick a wedding gift you really want, with returns and duplication avoided. Never again need newlyweds despair over seven toasters and sixteen cut-crystal fruit bowls.

Wedding gifts are traditionally addressed to the bride and sent to her parents' home. If the reception is at her parents' home, it is usual then for the presents to be forwarded to the parents' address prior to the wedding day.

China

Home entertaining plays a major part in most people's lives, and newlyweds want to be correct hosts. Despite today's relaxed approaches to table setting, it is wise to consider your future needs; be practical as well as creative.

Twentieth-century simplicity has replaced Victorian and Edwardian complexity at the table. The basic requirement in dinnerware is a five-piece place setting, which consists of the essential pieces in any pattern. These are:

dinner plate   bread-and-butter plate

A collection of English, American, Indian, Russian, and Chinese silver goblets surrounds an eighteenth-century Spanish colonial polychromed wood cherub in this opulent setting for a family dinner after the wedding reception on the stoa of Mr. and Mrs. Elton Hyder's Fort Worth, Texas, home. The antique vermeil flatware is by Odiot in Paris, the antique Imariware plates are English. The "Nemours" champagne flutes and silver salts and peppers are from Tiffany & Co.

dessert plate (also used for salad or
first course)

cup and saucer (counting as two pieces)

The balance of the service will consist of things such as:

soup plates

after-dinner-coffee cups and saucers

bouillon cups

Flat, open-type soup plates are ideal for serving pasta, or dishes which are fairly liquid, like moules marinières. Bouillon cups for clear soups are perfect also for desserts served with whipped cream or ice cream and berries. Be realistic about how many place settings you are going to need to begin with. Six or eight may suffice, and you can add later. China at good stores is labeled to show what the composition is—earthenware, stoneware, porcelain, bone china and so on; whether or not the pattern is dishwasher-safe and/or ovenproof. Generally speaking, an underglaze decoration is dishwasher-proof, while an overglaze pattern requires more delicate handling. Since gold is usually applied as an overglaze, it risks being removed by the action of an automatic dishwasher.

Besides basic dinnerware and a coffee or tea set, you must consider an assortment of china with particular uses:

serving platters (round, oval, elongated:
for chops or canapés; for meats and
for fish)

soup tureen

sauceboats

pitchers

vegetable dishes (open and covered)

breakfast sets

And add to your list those decorative and useful items which create atmosphere, such as vases, candlesticks, and cachepots.

"China" is the popular term for pottery, although the Greeks had the first and more accurate word with "ceramics" (*keramikos*). Brides confronted with choices that range from faience (earthenware with thick, colored glazes) to porcelain (the finest pottery made) tend to be confused. A rule of

Teaspoon   *Iced Tea Spoon*   *Dessert Knife*   *Lemon Fork*

Luncheon Fork   *Salad Fork*   *Fish Fork*   *Olive Fork*

Luncheon Knife   *Cake Server*   *Fish Knife*   *Roast Carver*

thumb decrees: don't mix thin, hard china with thick, softer ceramics; don't mix earthenware and faience with bone china and porcelain. Pottery is divided into four broad categories:

Earthenware: Straightforward clay, mixed with little else. Heavy, porous and opaque, it is made into many decorative/functional pieces; covered with glazes to render it waterproof, and fired at a low temperature. Earthenware for everyday use is relatively inexpensive, but less durable than other types of pottery. Its low firing temperature allows for a range and brilliance of color unavailable in other ceramics.

Stoneware: Clay, usually mixed with ground feldspar (a crystalline rock), is fired at a high temperature so that the additive becomes vitrified, and the vessel acquires the hardness of stone. Heavy, opaque and nonporous, it is used for pitchers, vases, and large platters as well as for dinnerware. Mason's "Ironstone" and Wedgwood's "Basalt" are popular examples of stoneware.

Porcelain: A fine, hard, translucent material made from kaolin (white china clay) quartz and feldspar and fired at high temperatures for vitrification. It is the hardest and most brittle of ceramics and, like glass, may be extremely thin.

Bone china: Porcelain with the addition of animal bone ash. This results in a white ware with a warm translucence, but slightly more opaque and less "vitreous" than true porcelain. Bone china is associated with English styles just as porcelain is associated with French, German, and Oriental styles and faience with Italian, Spanish, and Portuguese styles.

Before choosing a ceramic type, take time out to think about your lifestyle: where and how you will live. Will it be in the country or town? Do you like formal or informal gatherings? Traditional, country, or contemporary? French or English styles? Patricia Kennard, manager of Tiffany's Bridal Registry, says, "Your table setting can be operatic or playful. It helps customers if you point out that there are four basic design categories: floral, geometric, banded, and Oriental." An all-white set of porcelain or bone china is never a mistake in furnishing the china cupboard. You can mix patterns with solid colors or all-white, provided you do not mix porcelain with earthenware.

Dessert Spoon

Butter Spreader, Flat

Butter Spreader, H.H.

Cold Meat Fork

Gravy Ladle

Serving Fork

Steak Knife, Ind.

Berry Spoon

Butter Server

Roast Fork

Salad Serving Fork

Salad Serving Spoon

One creative way to start your china closet off is to select two basic but compatible patterns which, combined, produce a more interesting effect than simply matching everything on the table. For example, cobalt blue, orange, and gold Imari-type soup plates sit well on a blue-and-gold-banded dinner service, with perhaps the coffee cups and saucers repeating the floral design. All Empire or Louis XVI style designs sit well on plain white and gold-rimmed porcelain. A country-in-town effect for city apartments might be all-floral bone china but in different Indian, Chinese, or Japanese-inspired flower patterns, sharing a dominant color for harmony and balance.

Porcelain dinnerware can be very opulent and grand, with designs reproducing eighteenth- and nineteenth-century patterns which once graced the formal tables of the European courts. Earthenware tends to be more relaxed, yet its designs too can be centuries old and as intricate as porcelain designs, although the basic "drawing" of patterns will always be heavier; yet colors may be more refined than those of porcelain.

Crystal

Fine crystal adds sparkle to table settings. The stately dimensions of long-stemmed wine goblets will mate perfectly with traditional china and flatware patterns. Plain but graceful stemware will meld with less formal and contemporary designs. Stemware and barware represent the two basic types of glassware for drinking. There are also crystal giftwares, which encompass bowls, vases, candlesticks, and paperweights as well as crystal dinnerware, dessert and salad bowls, and finger bowls.

Although "crystal" is a term commonly used, it is also commonly misused. Glass, as opposed to crystal, is composed of sand, potash, soda, and lime. To qualify as crystal, lead oxide is substituted for the potash and soda, and there must be a minimum content of 16 percent lead. Full lead crystal contains 24 to 32 percent lead. When you compare glass to crystal, a distinct color difference is apparent; crystal is clearer, brighter, without the blue or greenish cast that often occurs in plain glass.

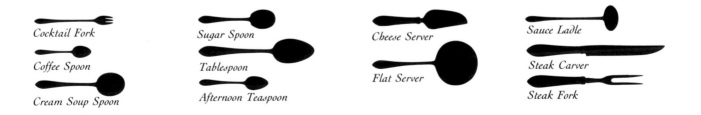

Cocktail Fork	*Sugar Spoon*	*Cheese Server*	*Sauce Ladle*
Coffee Spoon	*Tablespoon*	*Flat Server*	*Steak Carver*
Cream Soup Spoon	*Afternoon Teaspoon*		*Steak Fork*

Hand-blown crystal has faint variations that distinguish it from the machine-made product: an occasional trapped air bubble; a faint "thread" where the glass changed temperature while being washed. These are not imperfections but the unmistakable signs of genuine hand-blown glass.

Stemware and barware are offered plain and in patterns. Stores will stock stemware for a variety of purposes; a traditional crystal place setting consists of:

water goblet   claret (red wine glass)

white wine glass   champagne flute

Sherry glasses, brandy snifters, and liqueur glasses can be added later. A champagne flute will better preserve those precious bubbles, and takes up less space than the saucer-shaped champagne glass, which today is used more frequently for ice cream.

The basic barware shapes are:

single old-fashioned glass   highball glass (useful for mixed drinks,

double old-fashioned glass   iced tea, etc.)

Your barware may be a different pattern from your stemware, since they are not on the table together as a rule. Registering for sets of both plain and fancy glasses makes sense in terms of versatility. Stemware for specific wines, such as Rhine wines or burgundies, is another consideration for wine connoisseurs, and remember to list water pitchers and decanters.

Flatware

Silver has been prized as a precious metal second only to gold throughout history, its possession associated with prestige, power, and wealth. In the days before banks guarded our money, people hoarded silver coins which they then converted into knives, spoons, and grand serving pieces for display to demonstrate their standing in the community. Today there are few people who do not have some article—if only teaspoons—made of silver.

Dinner Fork   *Bouillon Spoon*   *Ice Tongs*   *Sugar Tongs*

Dinner Knife   *Dessert Fork*   *Jelly Spoon*   *Vegetable Spoon*

The silver used for flatware and hollow ware—silver vessels, trays, ice buckets and the like—is sterling silver. That is, 925 parts pure silver, made more durable by the addition of 75 parts copper. All articles stamped "sterling" must contain this percentage by law. Fine-quality sterling silver flatware is invariably finished by hand, which makes it an expensive but worthwhile investment for those who covet its warm luster and who care about balance, proportion, and subtlety of detail.

There is also a wide variety of brushed stainless steel flatware on the market; good-looking, dishwasher safe, and often with innovative, functional design.

A traditional five-piece place setting of flatware, whether sterling silver or stainless steel, consists of:

luncheon knife	dessert spoon
luncheon fork	butter knife
teaspoon	

A bride-to-be can begin her important silver flatware service with just four luncheon-sized place settings, and add more later. You will eventually graduate to large dinner knives and forks, fish knives and forks, and useful serving pieces. Remind friends and relatives which pattern you have chosen, and request pieces as birthday and holiday presents.

There is also a broad range of additional pieces; much depends on your lifestyle:

cocktail fork	bouillon spoon
iced tea spoon	salad fork
steak knife	coffee spoons

Serving Pieces:

serving spoons	sugar tongs
cheese scoops	berry spoons
ice tongs	cake server
salad servers	jelly spoon
sauce and soup ladles	steak fork and carver

Silver Care

People who turn away from sterling silver as requiring too much care are surprised at how simple it is to keep silver gleaming. There is a special silvercloth kit on the market to line the flatware drawer, with flaps to drop over the silverware and prevent tarnish. Silver used frequently tarnishes less. Wash it by hand in hot, sudsy water, and dry with a soft cloth. A reputable, preferably cream, silver polish is better than liquid "dip" polishes, which contain harsh chemicals. Cleaning tricks using aluminum foil, salt, or baking soda are strongly discouraged. Vermeil flatware should never be polished. It requires only washing in mild soapy water and drying well.

Vermeil

Nowadays vermeil for domestic use takes the form of flatware, centerpiece bowls, and candlesticks. Vermeil ware has a thin layer of gold over sterling silver, which gives the rich appearance of a solid gold article without the cost. It is an age-old process which reached its peak of popularity and refinement at the French courts of the seventeenth and eighteenth centuries, when demand for extravagant display of wealth was at its height. Nobles in those chaotic times thought it more prudent to own vermeil rather than something of solid gold, since valuable pieces in private hands were never safe from the grasp of the royal tax collectors.

Vermeil is wholly resistant to tarnish; however, it is a rather fragile finish, and vermeil flatware and hollow ware are not intended for everyday use.

The very ideal of a wedding chapel, this unique Meissen porcelain steepled church in the collection of Mrs. Dean Day Smith in Atlanta was modeled by Johann Gottlieb Ehder in 1748 as part of an entire miniature village made for Count Heinrich von Bruehl, then director of Augustus III of Saxony's Meissen porcelain manufactory.

Silver Hollow Ware

The finest sterling silver hollow ware is handmade and embraces long-standing traditions of craftsmanship and design. Domestic English silver, especially Georgian, has had the most influence on the styles of hollow ware used in America today. Bowls, coffeepots, pitchers and the like are fashioned from a sheet of silver worked over a perpetually turning, shaped wooden block, in a technique called spinning. The plain bodies are then finished with hand-applied decoration, which may involve engraving, etching, chasing, and applied ornamentation. In certain cases, such as candlesticks or paperweights, the entire article may be cast. All quality silver articles bear a stamp, or hallmark, with the maker's logo, name, or initials and the word "sterling."

Bed Linens

Serene, romantic, luxurious comfortable, practical; we demand it all of our beds and bedrooms nowadays. For many couples, the bedroom doubles as a media room, so leisure hours are added to sleeping hours, which necessitates serious thought about firm, back-supporting pillows as well as the decorative ones we love.

Modern brides may want the finest, which means mainly European, linens for their household trousseau. They are the impeccable, old-style kind woven from natural fibers, which Americans once traveled to Europe's capital cities to buy. Over the last decade or so, most leading European manufacturers have opened branches in the United States, bringing to our doorstep exquisite linens for bedroom, bathroom, and dining room.

Before registering for your linen trousseau, an explanation of the difference between the very best quality and the easy-care bed linens will help you decide. Muslin sheets are a blend of cotton and polyester, medium weight, with a no-iron, permanent press finish. Percale sheets are lighter and smoother, made of cotton treated for easy care. One hundred percent cotton sheets "breathe" and feel good against the skin: cooling in summer and healthier in winter. The finest for comfort, durability, and softness is Egyptian cotton, which after several washings tends to become silkier. The fibers originate in Egypt and the cloth is woven in France, Italy, Switzerland and other parts of Europe for high-quality men's shirting, ladies' blouses, and bed linens. Judged by the number of threads per square inch of fabric, the best Egyptian cotton has a staggering 320 count. Superior

A trousseau of bath linens and accessories from New York's Ad Hoc Housewares is shown with Fernando Sanchez bathrobes in this contemporary neoclassic bathroom designed by Arthur E. Smith.

The shower area of the mirrored bath features a first-century A.D. Roman head.

One of Fernando Sanchez's robes of his signature fabric (cotton blended with polyester in a moiré finish simulating watered silk) sits on a bronze stool by Diego Giacometti.

gauge has about 220 to 260. The higher the thread count, the stronger the fabric will be in terms of greater wearability. Good percale sheets have a thread count of 180 to 220. Quality all-cotton bed linen will require some light hand pressing to keep it looking good. America's manufacturers produce well-designed, hard-wearing bed linens in an enormous variety of colors, patterns, and moods. Traditional European linens are found only at more specialized showrooms, which may or may not have a bridal registry but which usually offer a personal service to brides. Familiar and famous: Léron, Pratesi, Porthault, and Frette are companies which have established a niche in American taste.

To dress a bed, your basic needs are:

3 sets of sheets (fitted and flat)	2 winter-weight blankets
6 sets of pillowcases	2 thin blanket covers
1 washable zip-on underslip per pillow	1 bedspread
1 dust ruffle	1 duvet
1 comforter	2 duvet covers
2 summer-weight blankets	1 mattress pad

Add an electric blanket, and any number of decorative pillows and pillow shams to your list. Contemporary interior designers have also reintroduced Americans to European square pillows (26 inches), with lace or frilly shams.

The Bathroom

Your bathroom should be dressed to coordinate with the décor of your bedroom, so when you register for your bathroom linens be specific. Do you prefer colored or plain; patterned or appliquéd; terry cloth or velour bath towels (which tend to be slightly less absorbent than terry cloth)? Here is a checklist to cover your basic bathroom needs:

3 bath towels (per person)	4 bathmats
3 hand towels (per person)	6 fingertip towels
6 facecloths (per person)	

Add beach towels, two sets of guest towels, bath sheets, and bathroom accessories to your list, as extras.

Table Linens

Table linens augment the drama of your table setting, unifying china patterns, centerpiece and, ultimately, the foods you will be serving. Dazzling white linen damask tablecloth and napkins are still the quintessential approach to a truly elegant dinner party. They should be used with tall candlesticks (light shed from a height is more flattering to a diner's face than light from below), fresh flowers, fine porcelain, good crystal, and sterling silver flatware.

There are a myriad different approaches to dressing a table, or even to setting a tray if viewing the VCR on occasion while you dine at home is what you like to do.

Fine cotton tablecloths and napkins in Provençal prints or gingham checks will give you a French country feeling; pastel colors mixing solids and stripes will speak of summer terraces everywhere; appliquéd organdy and you could be in Italy; chintzes or lace and it is Victorian England. Remember that food and wine spills make silks, brocades, and taffetas impractical for the dining table.

A lace-bordered cloth should not drop to the floor, for obvious reasons, but a full drop is glamorous for special occasions. A cloth that barely goes over the table's edge can look rather deprived. Measure the table and add 14 to 18 inches all around for a good fall that won't tangle with the guests' ankles.

Table mats are made from lace, plain fabric, cork, lacquered wood, rattan strips, dyed woven hessian, or plastic. Match mats with napkins, or play with contrasting ones. Paper napkins should be saved for children's parties only.

A pair of polished mahogany tea trays set with linen table mats and generous linen napkins will vastly upgrade your romantic at-home supper-on-a tray evenings together.

A basic table dressing list for your linen cupboard is:

1 best tablecloth: linen, cotton and linen, antique or modern lace, with matching napkins (set of no fewer than eight)	2 sets of eight matching or contrasting napkins
2 tablecloths in cotton or cotton blend (easy-care)	2 sets of eight table mats Assorted sets of table napkins

A word of explanation about damask: it is a white or monochrome, reversible figured textile where the pattern is formed by the two faces of the same "satin" weave.

Housewares

So much of what we use in the home links us to a rich and distant past. It is largely in the kitchen area that the technological age of the twentieth century steps in, with cookware and electrical appliances streamlined for looks and function, and major appliances like stoves and refrigerators now electronically controlled.

Microwave ovens and food processors have become part of the kitchen's equipment, and revolutionary improvements in stoves offer optimum cooking choices. For example, there are microthermal cooking ranges which incorporate a full-sized oven that can be programmed to microwave, can bake by radiant heat, or do both in combination. Cooktops with downdraft grills have become a standard feature in good-quality stoves.

Refrigerators not only match the décor with interchangeable laminated fronts, but are designed with chill and freeze areas for specific foods, ice makers, and wine storage compartments set at the correct temperatures for white and red wines.

It is perfectly logical to register for a professional stove, such as the famous Garland, if you are a serious cook. Remember that they cost as much again to install correctly, and your kitchen floor must be checked for strength—professional stoves can weigh over 800 pounds.

For your cookware registry the range is prodigal. A sampling for good cooks to consider: the Italian Alessi Company's 23-piece cook set in stainless steel, copper-clad and/or black iron; Le Creuset of France's enamel-coated cast-iron cookware is still the best of its kind; old-fashioned copper pans lined with tin or nickel silver—these are expensive but wear well, and are the choice of professional chefs.

Here is a useful kitchen checklist for shower or wedding gifts:

teakettle	soufflé dishes
pie tins	set of flat gratin dishes
gelatin molds	set of mixing bowls

For newlyweds who like to cook, Madeline Poley and Francine Scherer of the old Soho Charcuterie professionally equip a kitchen with a small industrial range, stainless steel wire shelving, and a butcher block counter. Cookware includes Calphalon and copper skillets, copper pots and a Tiffany silver saucepan, pitcher, and teapot. Blue and white porcelain mugs, a blue and yellow "Bigouden" porcelain cachepot holding bread, and the covered crystal bowls used to store beans and eggs are all from Tiffany's.

metal strainers	set of lidded saucepans
bulb baster	two sauté pans
kitchen timer	covered sauté pan
rolling pin	omelet pan
chopping boards	steamer
biscuit cutters	wok and stirrer
baking and roasting pans	bain-marie (double boiler)
graters	fish kettle
wire racks	Dutch oven
large fabric forcing bag with nozzles	ovenproof and flameproof casseroles
colanders	microwave cookware
flameproof ramekins	kitchen knives and tools
mortar and pestle	ice-cream maker (hand or electric)
polythene freezer-storage bins	pitchers

Electrical appliances:

hand-held egg beater/whisk	electric skillet
stand-mounted food processor	wall-mounted tin opener
blender	electric wok and tools
juicer	toaster
coffee grinder	coffee maker
espresso coffee machine	toaster oven
microwave oven	

Cookbooks and books on table setting and entertaining are also welcome gifts.

Video/Stereo

Media equipment is a new addition to the bridal registry. Most people already own a color television and stereo cassette and record player. This is an opportunity to upgrade and supplement your media room, but be sure to detail the make and type of equipment you want:

television with enlarged picture projection/stereo sound	portable mini-television
tv monitor and videocassette player	cam-recorder (video and sound movie camera)
video projector and screen	radio/cassette player
compact disc player	

The Esoteric Registry

Second- and third-time marrieds with established households may want to register for small-scale antiques. In New York there is even a registry at Manhattan's Sherry-Lehmann wine store for oenophiles. Stocking a good wine cellar is, after all, part of the good life.

THE BRIDAL SHOWER

Once the official engagement party has confirmed the good news, the whirl of shopping expeditions and bridal showers begins. The bridal "shower" was probably brought to America by early Dutch colonials, since the custom barely exists in Britain or France. In Holland, legend tells of a lovely maiden and an impoverished miller who fell in love and wished to marry. But her father disapproved and refused his daughter a dowry. So the sympathetic villagers came to their rescue and "showered" the bride with a multitude of household gifts.

It follows that showers are given by friends and/or working colleagues, rather than relatives. They take place some six weeks to a month before the wedding day. The main shower is likely to be given by the maid or matron of honor, with the bridesmaids' help, and even the groom is invited along. Delicious finger foods, punch or wine, and your friends' chance to demonstrate some token of their support to the future household will make the occasion a hit. Gifts are either of a general nature such as kitchenware, cookbooks, and similar items, money gifts in the form of a check or gift certificate, or something more personal from those close to the bride, such as lingerie for her trousseau. Some showers have themes, like a gardening tools or a stereo and CD accessories theme. Some guests avail themselves of the bride and groom's registered list at speciality stores.

Whatever kind of shower your devoted intimates, office or club acquaintances give you, the presents should be useful and modestly priced. And imaginative—otherwise the customary whoops of laughter and delight that generally accompany the opening of shower gifts will be missing.

*T*he great French animal sculptor
Edouard Marcel Sandoz in 1918 de-
signed this proto-Art Deco tête-à-tête
set with its duck-shaped pot, cream
pitcher, and sugar bowl. Its youthful
chic and wit have ensured the popu-
larity of this useful triumph of twen-
tieth-century giftware design made
exclusively for Tiffany's in Limoges
by Theodore Haviland from the origi-
nal Sandoz molds.

The Baccarat "Dyonisos" decanter
and covered silver beaker are of
Tiffany design.

Household linens and houseware ideas have already been suggested; here are some other items to consider:

china candlesticks	glazed terra-cotta soup bowls
hors d'oeuvre plates	cheese serving board
silver bar tools	breakfast tray
kitchen clock	tea cloths
cookery book stand	wastebin
oven mitts	bathroom accessories
home office accessories	

THE PREMARITAL AGREEMENT

Is the premarital agreement calculating? Or cynical? Hardly the case in this day and age of second and third marriages, or first-time marrieds who happen also to be top executives with accumulated assets to consider. In fact, a premarital agreement (called for convenience a PREMA) is the most useful tool that a couple can share.

PREMAs have been used for years by wealthy families to protect legitimate heirs, such as children from previous marriages or dependent relatives, and limit the otherwise powerful rights under law of a second or third spouse. In extended families, a PREMA acts as an insurance against divorce or the death of one of the couple.

To draw up a PREMA, each partner must be represented by an attorney. Since it is a legal contract, the couple must give their true financial picture. With a PREMA, property and assets owned by the partners prior to marriage can revert back to them in the case of divorce, and anything accrued during marriage by the shared efforts of both can be equally divided. A PREMA will invoke a fair settlement in cases such as extreme disparity in ages or the wealth of the couple; therefore *both* their interests are protected.

A small lunch for four—the couple and their respective lawyers—is an appropriate setting for the signing of the PREMA.

Attorney Joseph P. Zwack, in his authoritative book *Premarital Agreements*[*] cautions: ". . . there is a danger that a contract providing for disposal of assets . . . might tend to become a self-fulfilling

[*] Joseph P. Zwack, *Premarital Agreements* (New York: Harper & Row, 1987).

prophecy for a young couple marrying for the first time . . . I just wouldn't want to think about it if I had no reason to."

If you are approaching marriage with assets real enough, consider a PREMA. If you are entering marriage with certain doubts, consider a PREMA. They have been utilized in cases where the new spouse may wish to limit his or her responsibilities toward stepchildren. Some people have even chosen, perhaps humorously but probably from necessity, to have visits with in-laws confined to twice a year. It is important that bride and groom think through the veils of love and touch the reality of what they will or will not do. Depending on how creative and honest two people are in their thoughts, a PREMA can promise a better understanding of their shared future.

THE FATHER'S GIFT

Among the many thoughtful wedding traditions is the father's gift to his soon-to-be-married daughter. As an expression of lasting affection, a piece of fine jewelry is ideal; the classic choice, a good string of pearls. There is something in the purity of a pearl that confirms a father's feelings about his daughter. And their timelessness makes them important as a marriage gift.

Natural pearls, unless they are old ones offered for resale, are all but nonexistent today. High-quality cultured pearls are virtually indistinguishable from natural pearls and are formed, as every schoolgirl knows, in the same manner. A small irritant—say, a tiny piece of shell—is introduced artificially into the oyster mantle. This becomes coated over time with nacre (mother-of-pearl) and forms a pearl. Cultured pearls come primarily from the waters around Japan and are harvested like any crop; no two are exactly alike.

It takes an expert to judge a good pearl. The customer can perceive size, roundness, color, and how well matched the pearls are. The other criteria are luster and orient. Luster refers to the layers of nacre that give the pearl its appearance; orient (or overtone) is its translucent, rainbow effect. Whatever a pearl's body color, it should appear to come from deep within. The finest are pinkish white or silver-pink, although pearls occur in pastel shades of every hue.

Types of pearls are: baroque, mabé, freshwater, and Biwa freshwater. A baroque pearl is irregularly shaped, with dramatic ridges and protrusions. It is especially prized for pendants. A mabé pearl is a distinctive half or three-quarter round. It develops from a hemispherical nucleus implanted on the inside of the oyster shell. The nacre coating forms a deeply iridescent blister, which is the pearl.

Their half-dome shape lends them readiness for setting into lustrous pins or earrings. Freshwater pearls are the "Rice Krispies" of the pearl pantheon, and are cultured using a small piece of tissue rather than a fragment of shell or bead. Thus they are non-nucleus pearls, produced by the humble mussel in lakes and rivers. Biwa pearls come from Lake Biwa in Japan, and are cultured using freshwater clams. Irregular in shape and of excellent color, they require three years to mature and are the finest of their kind.

The pearl is the birthstone for the month of June and the ancients assigned it powers to promote health and long life.

WEDDING BUDGET

Who lavishes this wedding upon this bride and groom? Several persons may and indeed do, but for the majority of first-time weddings the lion's share is still paid for by the bride's parents. This speaks of more than propriety; in the hearts and minds of the nation's families it is old-fashioned, loving pride. Their daughter is taking a big step, and to demonstrate their support they will want to give her an incomparable wedding day.

The occasion is no less momentous for the groom and his family, who may offer to share the financial burden. The bride's parents can gratefully decline, if they so wish. If the big day is planned as a collaborative effort, with a cost contribution from both sets of parents and the bride and groom, it is wise to settle beforehand how bills will be allocated. In this case you might appoint someone as treasurer—one of the parents, or a sister or brother, in order to keep things on track. The traditional breakdown of expenses follows. The bride's parents pay for:

invitations and announcements

bride's wedding costume and personal
    trousseau

decorations, attendants' bouquets and
    flowers

professional photography

church fees

transportation

reception, including all rentals and
    gratuities

accommodation for out-of-town
    bridesmaids

The bride (or her parents) may buy the groom's ring and his wedding gift; her personal stationery, and the gifts for her attendants. The groom or his family pays for:

the bride's engagement and wedding rings	corsages for the mothers and
marriage license and officiator's fee	grandmothers
groom's clothes	wedding gift for bride
ushers' dress accessories	gifts for best man and ushers
bride's bouquet and corsage	accommodation for out-of-town ushers
boutonnières for groom and male	honeymoon trip
attendants	

Bridesmaids, best man, and ushers pay for their own outfits and any traveling expenses, as a rule.

Since circumstances for every couple differ, there is no absolute law as to who picks up the tab. A wedding can be paid for by any interested party—a magnanimous aunt, a wealthy friend—as well as by the bride and groom. Budget discussions mean decisions must be made on the size, and formality or informality of your wedding. You can settle for something small, smart, and very formal; or on an elaborate spectacular. The depth of your or your parents' pocketbook is relevant; however, many families are willing to splurge for the event. Second- and third-time weddings have tended to become as lavish as the first, which explains why the best professionals in the business are so busy. So for a large, traditional wedding of 300 to 400 guests, you must plan at least one year ahead. A less formal affair might take six months' preparation.

SETTING THE DATE AND LOCATION

The where and the when of your wedding day is a primary decision, dependent on your faith, background, and lifestyle. For many centuries in England and other parts of Europe, couples were wedded at the church door, for to marry inside the church was thought to be sacrilegious. Since a wedding was often a riotous event which involved an entire village or local community, it was very much a public affair. Following the service, the new husband would be openly presented with his bride's dowry, thus making common knowledge of its value to the great satisfaction of both families. By the mid-sixteenth century, bride and groom could be happily united before the altar, and "church porch" weddings passed into history. Today, the majority of first-time marrieds want their union

For a home wedding, a living room is transformed into a wedding chapel with an exuberant use of fresh greens woven with silk ribbons, red roses, and candles. Fort Worth interior designer Ken Blasingame, who decorated the event in this casual, romantic, and lavish way, says, "I like overdoing for a wedding party. If people can't see it all at once, it keeps them amused."

solemnized in a house of worship, wondrously decked out in traditional trappings, and with every ancient rite and practice in place.

If you are affiliated with your local church or synagogue, the decision is simple; however, you may still have to book the wedding up to one year in advance, especially if you live in a big city or suburb. The officiator counsels you both upon the liturgy, and upon any personal vows you may wish to include. If one partner is of another religious denomination, it may be possible to combine the rituals of both faiths in an ecumenical service.

A prominent Protestant cleric, Dr. David Read of the Madison Avenue Presbyterian Church in New York City, offers the wisdom of over thirty years' experience: "Christian marriage is for anyone who is willing to accept the *Christian* view of marriage, and desires the blessing of God. Which means that it is not a civil contract, but a religious one, and for life. You don't have to be a member of this or any other church, so long as you can demonstrate your belief in this concept." Dr. Read is unenthusiastic about new forms of expression in the traditional marriage service, preferring the beauty of language from older books of worship: "Young people nowadays ask me for the full-blown ceremony of their forebears. Marriage and the birth of a child are two life events that break the crust of agnosticism which generally affects the younger generation. After this, they begin to sense the mystery of life."

The Catholic church requires a premarital instruction period between the priest and couple, lasting about six months prior to the wedding day. If the couple are both Catholic, the banns (announcing their intention to marry) are "called" in the parish churches of each. That is, an announcement is made from the pulpit at Mass on three consecutive Sundays before the wedding; or they may be published in the church bulletin. If one of the partners is non-Catholic, banns are not usually required.

A full Catholic wedding involves the celebration of Mass and Nuptial Blessing, and must be held within a church or chapel. However, a couple can decide upon a simple marriage service without a

The small, picturesque, and typically American Neo-Gothic stone chapel of Saint Columba built in 1885 in Middletown, Rhode Island, is distinguished by Louis Comfort Tiffany windows. In front of the richly *colored Tiffany glass, the altar is decorated for an afternoon wedding with an expansive arrangement of pink peonies and roses in "The Pueblo Bowl," made of silver inlaid with copper and niello by Tiffany's.* *Newport florist Jean E. Gorham of Green Schemes extends her central bouquet with more pink and white flowers and vines attached to the tall wrought-iron cardholders that flank the altar.*

Mass. If the marriage is interfaith, a Mass may be held as long as the non-Catholic is a baptized Christian, although he or she will not be offered Communion. In other respects, the Catholic service is similar to the Protestant. The custom of giving the bride away is deleted from the Catholic procedure: the father will escort the bride to the altar, kiss her, and return to his seat. Today at Protestant ceremonies it is usual for the father to respond, when the question "Who giveth this bride . . . ?" is asked, "Her mother and I do."

The Jewish wedding ceremony has its base in the entire culture, and the strong traditions of the Jewish heritage render marriage a communal, as well as a personal and spiritual event. Each of the different branches of the Jewish faith, Orthodox, Conservative, and Reform, has its variations on the service. Jews can be married outside of the synagogue so long as the setting is appropriate. At the ceremony, the bride and groom are escorted by their respective parents to stand before the rabbi beneath the *chuppah*. The *chuppah*, a small canopy raised on poles, symbolizes the tent in which in ancient times newlyweds would isolate themselves for a period, as protection against evil. A sip of wine is taken, and the couple receive the first blessing. The groom gives the bride a plain gold ring and presents her with a marriage contract called the *Ketubah*. A new liberal attitude allows an exchange of wedding rings between Jewish couples, who want to show that their commitment is mutual. Speak to your rabbi about this, keeping in mind that the Orthodox ceremony does not condone it. There is a further taking of wine and the Seven Blessings are bestowed, followed by the ceremonial breaking of the wineglass, thought to remind those assembled of the fragility of life. In conclusion, for the Orthodox, the couple retires to a private room for a while, to signify the consummation of the marriage and to share a little food together (and to break their day's fast). As every young Jewish pledged couple knows, the feasting, music, and dance that follow a wedding are an unfettered, boundless, overwhelming expression of community joy that is all-pervading, and calls for stamina.

Your marriage ceremony can be held at home or anywhere else, provided something of the sacredness of the occasion is established. Whether civil or religious, you can wed on a mountaintop, in a garden, on board a yacht, at a hotel or country club. The ceremony has been performed everywhere from the bottom of a lagoon in scuba-diving gear, to a hot-air balloon, with bride, groom, and wedding party suspended in the basket. The more relaxed attitude of religious bodies toward interfaith and second and third marriages means that divorced couples too can be united at the altar with due pomp and ceremony.

A civil marriage can be performed by a justice of the peace, registrar, county clerk, town mayor, or the governor of the state. Civil ceremonies can be formal or informal; involve a large gathering followed by a flamboyant reception, or be entirely private with two legal witnesses.

Marriage licenses should be obtained at a courthouse in the state in which you are to be married. The clerk of courts will apprise you of all necessary requirements. Whether the service is civil or religious, it must conform to the laws of the state. You and your fiancé should bring the following documents when applying for a license: a doctor's certification verifying the results of your blood tests; your birth certificates and/or proof of citizenship; your divorce papers if remarrying; your parents' written consent if underage. Allow two or three days for the license to be processed; note that it is usually valid for thirty days.

FLOWERS AT THE CEREMONY

A wedding ceremony without flowers would be unthinkable. Flowers, herbs, and wheat were once strewn along the path of the bride, to link her progress with the symbolic blessings of nature. Today, the place of ceremony is rich with fragrant blooms, and the bride in her bouquet will carry lilies for purity, white roses for worth, baby's breath (in place of wheat) for fertility. The decoration of church, chapel, temple, or synagogue plays an important and often memorable role in the entire proceedings.

A professional floral designer will know the factors to consider. That churches have high ceilings is a given, which means tall flowers will scale better in the space. Imagine lofty stands of flowers at each end of the altar, long-stemmed varieties tied with ribbons at the end of each pew. Large-headed blooms such as peonies, chrysanthemums, or calla lilies are more easily seen by everyone in a spacious environment. However, the floral displays should not obstruct the guests' view of bride and groom taking their vows.

The traditional *chuppah* at a Jewish wedding is often fashioned as a glorious canopy or arch of fresh flowers, large enough to embrace bride, groom, their attendants, and even both sets of parents.

For a big wedding in New York, John Funt, Tiffany's talented Director of Interior Display, placed topiary trees the length of the aisle in the encircling Byzantine splendor of Saint Bartholomew's basilica on Park Avenue. "I like to use little trees for a sculptural effect. White flowers range from shell pink to cream to dead white; all of which exists in magnolias, for instance, which have magnificent depth and subtlety. I don't see why flowers should always be contrasted with green leaves. I prefer to have some stems of a deep color—say, garnet red roses—to set off the white flowers."

Weddings are invariably more pleasurable if they take note of seasonal changes. Professionals love to use dogwood and lilac in late spring and the peony's showy blooms at the height of summer.

Floral decorations for ceremonies at home can be bountiful in the extreme, and they come off better if planned to complement the bouquets carried by the bridal party. Two parallel lines of fully flowering shrubs, hired for the day, make an effective aisle, as do stands of flowers joined by satin ribbons. They can lead to a flower-decked home altar: a table laid with a cloth, plain or sumptuous, with religious paraphernalia flanked by two big candlesticks. There is greater creative freedom in the decoration of at-home ceremonies and receptions—a chance to make form and content more personal. New York florist Marlo Phillips, who once decorated the city's Knickerbocker Club for a formal wedding, transforming it into a fantasy Edwardian conservatory, says, "You shouldn't try to impose something too arbitrary on good period rooms. The Knickerbocker's architecture is turn-of-the-century, so an Edwardian setting made sense."

THE BRIDE'S DRESS

The magic begins: envision yourself floating down the aisle in a long dress of ancestral white, trailing rivers of lace, to the delighted gasps of the assembled crowd. It is a dream soon to become reality, a fact most brides appreciate when they pull some ravishing bridal creation over their heads in the silken hush of a bridal salon. Even the most sophisticated will marvel at the sight of themselves all decked out in wedding white.

Brides throughout the ages have worn every color, including green (Norway) and black (Iceland). In ancient Rome a bride wore a saffron-colored robe over her tunic, and over her padded coiffure a flaming orange veil. A wreath of myrtle and orange blossoms held the veil in place. White, the medieval symbol of virginity, was adopted by many Elizabethan brides as proof of their virtue. The wealthy women of Renaissance Italy preferred cloth of gold and rich velvets. In the eighteenth century brides sometimes wore elaborate white satin ball gowns, later to be put to good use for dances. It was the nineteenth century that established white as the bridal color once and for all, confirming the demure purity of the Victorian bride. And so it has remained in our own century, with a slight digression into pastel shades in the 1920s.

Fashion has played a large part in bridal wear: the season's dominant silhouette is reflected in bridal dresses and headgear. The tradition of closing a top couturier's spring and fall collections with a slam-bang bridal outfit has evolved over the past decade into couture-designed bridal lines. Famous names like Geoffrey Beene, Bill Blass, Oscar de la Renta, Carolina Herrera, Mary McFadden, Arnold Scaasi have turned their talents to dressing the modern bride. In wedding dresses, the ultimate fantasies, couturiers can demonstrate their brilliance at mixing fabrics and detail. The back of the gown, which is a focal point during the ceremony, receives attention with gathers, bustles, bows, back necklines plunging into deep Vs, or some other invention. Peplums; shoulder flounces; exorbitant amounts of tucks; layering; crystal and pearl beading; all go to make breathtakingly original creations.

Nostalgia has reintroduced Victorian and Edwardian styles: tight bodices above billowing skirts; puffed or leg-o'-mutton sleeves. The goal is to find what suits both your dream and your physical type. When you shop for *the* dress, take someone with you—your mother or a close friend. Make an appointment to talk with the bridal dress consultant, who will offer experienced and enthusiastic help. Bring a pair of satin pumps with you, and don't hesitate to try on a number of different dresses, headpieces and veils, to see the entire effect. Brides' and bridesmaids' dresses are custom-fitted, so you must allow three to four months for your order to arrive and for alterations to be made, especially in the busy season which now runs from April through December.

A second- or third-time bride planning a formal or semiformal wedding can dress as extravagantly as she cares to, although such ritual details as a full veil and train are usually dispensed with.

The style of your wedding, the time of year, your budget—all will involve you in many dizzying decisions. Heavy satins, velvets, or jacquards trimmed with lace, pearls, fur, or feathers are perfect choices for a winter event. Lighter silk-satins, paper and moiré taffetas, fine lawn or eyelet cottons will be cool and light for warmer months. Chiffon, organza, tulle, and Swiss voiles are fabrics which go over very fine cotton or silk. If you plan to wear an antique veil, perhaps a family heirloom, bring it to the bridal store to see how it combines with the dresses you will be trying on. In certain specialty stores you can find gowns made to order from layers of antique lace. Lace and ruffles are

pure romance, and both are used in abundance on wedding dresses. Modern lace is usually of two types:

Alençon—curving floral elements, distinctively outlined with cord on a net ground.

Chantilly—exuberant floral patterns on lacy or net ground.

What are the lengths and names of the different trains? They are:

Court train—extends 1 foot along floor

Chapel train—extends 1⅓ yards

Cathedral train—extends 2½ yards

A train longer than Cathedral is very formal, the kind that dazzles at royal weddings. A short train just sweeps the floor and looks glorious with a frothy, to-the-floor veil. Trains are also in different styles:

Attached—extends from the back of a long skirt

Capelet—falls from the shoulder

Detached—falls from the waist

Watteau or Sacque-back (eighteenth-century)—falls from the back yoke of a fitted-bodice dress

Veils are made in customary lengths:

Bouffant (to the shoulder)

Elbow

Fingertip

Ballerina or Walking (12 inches longer than fingertip)

Long (to ankle or floor)

For a country estate wedding Arnold Scaasi creates a poufed and tiered sleeveless gala wedding dress of white organza embroidered with white chalk sequins in an overall leaf pattern and decorated with sequined organdy roses.

The bride will dress in one of the French Provincial guest rooms of the Jordan Winery while admiring the panoramic view of the Alexander Valley and the splendid all-white bouquet of Queen Anne's lace, roses, madonna lilies, freesias, snapdra-

gons, and foxglove arranged by San Francisco florist Michael Daigian in a white bisque Tiffany "Tulip" pitcher.

Her scalloped white satin pumps are from Marina Morrison Ltd., also of San Francisco.

They can be doubled, trebled, scattered with pearls or sequins, or accented with ribbon streamers. Veils spring from headpieces to flatter your face, hairstyle, and dress. Choose from:

Bandeau	Crown
Bow	Diadem
Cap	Mantilla
Circlet	Snood
Comb	Wreath

Or have your hairdresser custom-braid a hairpiece entwined with artificial flowers, ribbons, and seed-pearl sprays.

Between the world wars, bridal costume veered between flapper, medieval, and convent styles. The 1940s brought in figure-hugging "Greek" styles in draped white silk jersey. Today novelty still abounds, with kicky flamenco dresses, the skirts ending in a deep flounce; big-shouldered, jacket-style tops encrusted with satin-ribbon spaghetti; off-the-shoulder, bare-backed, or even bare-midriff dresses to please a spirited young bride. Or you can choose to be stylishly informal: a street-length, silk-faced satin two-piece suit topped with a modish hat.

A sleeveless or short-sleeved dress calls for a pair of elegant long gloves. Keep in mind that they must be easily removable during the service, so that the ring can be put on your finger. Instead of a bouquet, you can hold a Bible or satin clutch purse, with flowers—lilies or orchids—pinned to it.

Pamper yourself at a beauty salon that offers a special six-month beauty package to brides: facials, body massage, hair treatments, manicures and pedicures, as well as lessons in makeup, the better to preen yourself for the great day. Make sure you have made your appointments for your makeup and hairdo on the morning of your wedding, and allow two hours in which to get dressed.

The family seamstress created this charmingly old-fashioned wedding dress for Mr. and Mrs. Elton Hyder's daughter Whitney's "at home" wedding in Fort Worth, Texas.

The dress's tiers of antique lace and satin ribbon are ornamented with tiny bouquets of pastel silk flowers from Paris.

Mrs. Hyder's pet soft-coated Irish wheaten terrier Astor looks on, festively coiffed with a hair ribbon.

THE BRIDE'S BOUQUET

There are several schools of thought about bridal bouquets; an armful of long-stemmed flowers tied with ribbons is one idea, a beautifully structured spray incorporating full blooms, buds, and leaves is another. Few bridal bouquets nowadays include rosemary for remembrance, sage for wisdom, and garlic to drive off evil spirits, but many still entwine ivy for fidelity and lily of the valley for lasting love. We care about the language of flowers the way our ancestors did, and think deeply about overall effect and the comfort of the bride. Only a young woman as statuesque as Britain's Princess of Wales can carry off the kind of mountainous bouquet of white flowers—mostly Mountbatten roses—and greenery which Lady Diana Spencer carried at her marriage to Prince Charles. The bouquet should match the image of the bride herself and what she is wearing: Long and unstructured for a willowy type with a gown to the floor; massed and full, perhaps, for a young woman of medium height in a ballerina-length dress; a Victorian nosegay for the truly petite. Each bride is different, and whether she is marrying for the first, second, or even third time, she wants a look that is romantic.

The well-known New York florist Renny Reynolds says: "A bouquet with a strong line becomes a continuation of the bride's arm, and is perfect if the dress is long-line also. We're presently making one with white freesias and leggy strands of dendrobium orchids, which looks loose, but is wired so that it holds together." This is closer in spirit to Edwardian bouquets, which were larger and looser than the Victorian ones, with ribbons reaching to the floor.

The flowers most loved for bridal bouquets are: roses, of many types and in color from white to pink to champagne; the waxy white stephanotis; the lily family, such as callas, rubrums, and the lily-like nerines; white irises; freesias; miniature gladiolus, and orchids, especially dendrobiums, cattleyas, and cymbidiums. Long-stemmed tulips from France, which tower over their Dutch brethren, fare well when swagged with thick ribbon into dramatic armfuls. Gardenias are stunning but fragile; they will turn brown before the end of a long day. Paper-white narcissus; daisies; sweet pea; Queen's Anne's lace—the large, cultivated kind; ixia, and miniature carnations are all ideally suited to bridal bouquets. The character of certain flowers and their arrangement can evoke nostalgia: big, cattleya orchids used alone are reminiscent of the fifties; a sheaf of calla lilies is pure 1930s Deco; a bunch of wildflowers and the bride in a caftan, what else but the 1960s?

Designing flower bouquets is an art. When ordering your bouquet at a good florist, go in person so that he or she can get a sense of you. Describe your dress, veil, and the kind of wedding you are planning. The florist knows that it must be well made, not only to last, but to stand up to the nervous grip of the bride. It must be kept light, because a heavy bouquet can make a bride look awkward. It must not be too large if the bride is short, or too small if the bride is Olympian. In sure hands, practical and beautiful are combined in formal, informal, romantic, or sophisticated fashion—in short, in whatever the bride might visualize for her great day.

Attendants' Flowers and Parents' Corsages

The majority of brides wish to carry white or pale-colored flowers, so the bridesmaids' bouquets offer an opportunity to play with color. For visual symmetry, their flowers should complement the bridal bouquet and ceremony flowers as a whole, then blend, match, or contrast with the bridesmaids' own dresses. The maid or matron of honor's bouquet is made in keeping with her outfit. Give your florist a complete description of the attendants' dresses, as well as the mothers' and grandmothers' costumes, so that he can plan the bouquets and corsages appropriately. For couples from divorced families, this is a nice moment to remember a corsage for the wife of your remarried father, and any stepsister who will be present.

Junior bridesmaids and flower girls are dressed to coordinate with the bridesmaids' gowns, but in younger styles and possibly different fabrics. Little girls are charming in short, ruffled dresses with fresh flowers in their hair. Their baskets can be filled with posies, bound with ribbons not so long as to trip them up.

Boutonnières

At weddings in the past, the male attendants and fathers—not the groom—used to wear a white carnation in their left buttonhole. The flower was ubiquitous, universally identified with a wedding and little used for anything else. In our time, the carnation has been replaced as a boutonnière by rosebuds, or sprigs of stephanotis or freesia. Yet in Persia the carnation was, and still is, the most prized flower. At a wedding, bride and groom carried them, wore them woven into crowns on their heads, and were pelted with them by their joyful friends. In our time, newer strains have brought the carnation back into favor, with the Chinese miniature, the larger heads and longer stems of the standard, and vibrant, dual-color types unimagined before.

Whatever the choice for the ushers' boutonnières, they should all wear the same flower. The best man may select his own, while the groom is expected to wear a blossom from the bride's bouquet. It is one of the best man's responsibilities to see that every man in the wedding party has a boutonnière.

THE GROOM'S CLOTHES

Men are more influenced by what is fashionable than they care to admit. And at their own wedding, few want to look anything but debonair. Drabness is out. Style, cloth, cut, and dash are most definitely in. The news item about a groom and his four ushers who were ". . . suited up in pastel tuxes" and wore Ray-Ban sunshades will convey just how hip young men can be.

Clothes etiquette for the groom, the male attendants, and the fathers is closely tied to the time of day of the wedding. The simplest explanation of what to wear follows:

Very formal daytime (before 6 P.M.)	Black or Oxford gray cutaway coat; striped trousers; gray waistcoat; dress shirt with wing collar; striped silk ascot; gray gloves; black shoes and socks. Silk top hats.
Very formal evening (after 6 P.M.)	Black tailcoat; black satin-trimmed trousers; white piqué waistcoat; stiff-front dress shirt with wing collar; white piqué bow tie; white gloves; black patent-leather shoes; black socks. Black silk top hat.
Formal daytime	Black or gray sack coat or stroller; striped trousers; gray vest; dress shirt; bow or striped tie; gray gloves; black shoes and socks. Homburg for a Jewish ceremony.
Formal daytime (contemporary)	Black or gray contoured long or short jacket; matching trousers; dress shirt with wing collar; bow tie; gray vest. Or formal suit in choice of colors and styles; white shirt; striped tie; vest or cummerbund.
Formal evening	Black or gray tuxedo or dinner jacket; matching trousers; dress shirt; vest or cummerbund; bow tie; black shoes and socks.
Formal evening (contemporary)	Tuxedo or dinner jacket in color of choice; matching or black trousers; dress shirt; vest or cummerbund; bow tie; black shoes and socks.

Informal daytime or evening	Black, gray, or dark blue suit; white or pastel-colored shirt; vest optional; bow or striped tie. Or, summer-weight jacket with white trousers. Or, white suit. Or, navy blue blazer with gray flannel trousers.

If our groom is an arbiter of taste, his tuxedo or cutaway might be designed by Geoffrey Beene, Oscar de la Renta, or Bill Blass. Which implies magic in the line, fabric, and details. If he wears a suit, it might be a Perry Ellis or Ralph Lauren design. Which implies texture and an up-to-the-minute contour. These are some of the designers who have taken men's formal wear and charged it with well-bred and luxurious innovation. And, in many cases, color.

With formal dress, the groom's jewelry should be a black or white pearl or gold stickpin and gold cuff links. Gold or silver set with colored stones can be worn with informal wear.

HER ATTENDANTS' CLOTHES

On the subject of bridesmaids' dresses, this amusing editorial is from a 1936 bridal issue of *House & Garden:* "It is extremely difficult for a brunette who is four feet eight inches tall to look her best in a frock and hat identical to one worn with great effect by a tall blonde. . . ." Our own top designers relish such a challenge. The bridesmaids' costumes take their cue from the bride's: If she is in a floor-length formal gown, their dresses should be long and formal also (and so on).

The bridesmaids' dresses can bring color to the all-white ceremony. Soft pastels and sherbets for a summer wedding pleases everybody; but imagine them in jewel-like colors, glowing in the dim interior of church or synagogue at a winter wedding. (Remember, blue shades turn gray in candlelight.)

After you have selected your own gown, have the maid or matron of honor involved when ordering the bridesmaids' outfits. She will help you choose pretty, matching dresses that are becoming to all. Since no six maids are going to agree about what they will wear, better that they entrust the decision to you. The maid or matron of honor may choose her own outfit, as long as it harmonizes with the general mood of the wedding.

At very formal events, the maids wear gloves. Their headpieces might be flowers in their hair, romantic hats, or caps made from silk rosebuds, beads, seed pearls, or lace. Accessories are kept fairly simple, and should either coordinate or be contrasted with the color of their dresses. It is the responsibility of the maid or matron of honor to see that the bridesmaids are on call for their fittings, wear shoes which blend with their dresses, and have their gloves, headpieces, and bouquets together an hour before the ceremony so that they can all help prepare the bride.

Flower Girls, Page Boys, and the Ring Bearer

Children are the most fun of all to dress. They love the idea and will readily accept the fanciest clothes, especially little girls. Keep their dresses short: ruffled pinafores over peeping petticoats; velvet dresses with huge satin sashes. Whichever you choose will look better with pantyhose and flat, button-strap shoes. The tinier boys will be beguiling in Eton-collared velvet suits or blue mini-blazers with white shorts and white knee socks. Older boys will appreciate long-trousered suits similar to the men's formal or informal wear.

Mothers' Wedding Clothes

The mothers of the bride and groom have major stature at a wedding; to some extent the pageant revolves around the couple and themselves. They may be the dual hostesses of the reception, very much on view, greeting guests on every side. Their attire can be more personal; mature, glamorous, unquestionably right.

At a formal wedding held during the daytime—that is, before 6 P.M.—the mothers wear street-length outfits. After 6 P.M. they can wear floor- or ballerina-length gowns. Add a smart hat, good jewelry, gloves, and the very portrait of motherly love and dignity is complete.

HIS ATTENDANTS' CLOTHES

Best man and ushers follow protocol and take their cue from the groom's attire. The chart for the groom applies to the men of the wedding party as well; however, the details should be varied so that the groom stands out. If the affair is very formal, the best man may wear a plain ascot to the groom's striped one, for example, while the ushers may all wear bow ties. Other points of variation can be in the waistcoats or cummerbunds, the dress shirts and the boutonnières. All will help indicate who everyone is.

The Fathers' Wedding Clothes

The fathers also wear formal attire, if they so desire. Again, the details can be varied. Only the men of the wedding party are expected to wear formal dress or tuxedos. Male guests wear suits or informal jackets and trousers, coordinated to whatever their female companions are wearing.

GIFT FOR ATTENDANTS

To express thanks for the loving, diligent care they receive, both bride and groom present their attendants with some small gift as a memento of their wedding day. The maid or matron of honor and best man generally receive a different, somewhat more extravagant token in appreciation of the extra duties they must perform. Otherwise, the bride usually gives all the bridesmaids the same gift; the groom will do the same with the ushers.

The bride can distribute her gifts at the bridesmaids' luncheon; the groom at the bachelor party, along with the ties and gloves he buys for the ushers' attire, or both sets of gifts can be given to the attendants at the rehearsal dinner. Below is a list of captivating things to consider. (Remember to allow three to four weeks extra for any objects you want to have engraved.)

For the bridesmaids	*For the ushers*
silver or gold earrings	gold cuff links
silver or gold pins	gold tie bar or stickpin
gold locket on chain	gold belt buckle
silver rope necklace or bracelet with gold twist	silver bar knife
silver powder compact	silver pocket flask
silver picture frame	silver money clip
cut-crystal powder box	leather stud box with initials in gold
cut-crystal perfume atomizer with silver stopper	crystal paperweight
heart-shaped key ring	set of 4 cut-crystal goblets
heart-shaped silver bookmark	cut-crystal decanter
hand-painted porcelain box	silver ball-point pen

THE BACHELOR DINNER

The bachelor dinner has a longer history than most of the prewedding parties. A night of camaraderie and carousing brought the novice groom together with his closest companions for some last-minute advice regarding the nuptial bed. Nowadays it is more likely to take the form of a dinner party hosted at home, in a restaurant, or club by the groom himself or one of his friends. Male friends and favorite male relatives attend, including the best man and ushers. The party takes place two or three days prior to the wedding, not on the night before, which is normally reserved for the rehearsal dinner.

At the bachelor dinner, the groom conveys his thanks to the best man and ushers and presents his gift to each, or saves this last gesture for the rehearsal dinner. In any case, the high spirits will have the quality of a last, wild night out even if nobody tumbles to the floor. Smashing the champagne glasses after the traditional toast to the bride is no longer considered very proper—a custom best left to history.

THE BRIDESMAIDS' LUNCHEON

The bridesmaids' luncheon, given by the bride for her attendants or by the attendants for the bride, is another little prewedding festivity. One of the mothers may offer to host the occasion at home, and close female relatives can be invited as well. The menu should have a light emphasis. A quaint old custom is to offer a cake, with pink sugar frosting, in which has been baked the following "charms": a dime (for wealth); a ring (for the next to be married), and a thimble (for her who will choose not to marry). The attendants, if they host, will wish to present the bride with the traditional bridesmaids' present—usually something fine for the household: a cut-glass crystal bowl, or a pair of silver wine coasters, for example. If the bride hosts, this is the right moment to thank the assembled ladies for their help with the wedding preparations, and to give her attendants their gifts.

GIFTS TO EACH OTHER

The exchange of wedding gifts between bride and groom is an old social convention in many lands. The Jewish women of Morocco, praised for their beauty by painters like Delacroix, gave their husband-to-be a belt with an incised silver buckle. In return, he presented her with a belt with an elaborate gold buckle. The gifts, with their symbolism of attachment, were worn on their wedding day.

His

A gift of jewelry—precious, portable, lasting, enhancing—has marked occasions of sentimental importance in this and every other age. Jewelry from her husband-to-be is something the bride will wish to wear on her wedding day. The groom can select from among a number of appropriate pieces:

aquamarine-and-diamond earrings (for something blue)
pearl bracelet with diamond clasp
diamond ear studs
diamond band bracelet
mabé pearl earrings

Hers

A young bride's choice for her groom is very often a gold watch. Or the couple may exchange His and Her watches. As tokens of sentiment, watches are generally engraved with the wedding date and the couple's initials. Other ideas for her gift to him are:

gold cuff links with matching studs (with or without semiprecious stones)
man's gold link bracelet
tiepin
set of men's luggage
engraved silver cigarette box
ivory- or silver-backed hairbrushes

Or, more extravagantly of course, you could exchange matching Mercedes sports cars.

THE CEREMONY AND THE MUSIC

Each couple's desires and circumstances will dictate the choice of a civil or religious ceremony. Seventy-five percent will elect to be married in a church, chapel, or synagogue. The aura of solemnity, the beauty of the space, fulfill for many a bride and groom the need for a setting that will truly sanctify their vows.

In a church, the seating arrangements are: the bride's family and friends sit on the left of the aisle during the ceremony; the groom's to the right. If the bride's parents are divorced and both remarried, the father will move from the altar to a second or third pew behind the mother's pew, where his new wife is seated. The stepfather will be in the mother's pew. If the bride lives with her father, and he and her stepmother are hosting the wedding, it is they who occupy the front left pew while the mother and her new husband, if any, sit behind them. Should an uncle, brother, or friend give the bride away, they will join the mother in her pew. The same configuration serves if the groom's parents are divorced and either of them remarried. If a grandmother or aunt is filling in for an absent or deceased mother of the bride, she will take the place of honor in the left front pew. Children of the marriage sit in these pews with their parents.

At a given signal, the groom and best man take their places with the clergyman, as the bride, her father, and the attendants form the processional in the vestibule. Meanwhile two of the younger ushers will be rolling out the canvas aisle carpet, if one is used, and two others affixing the pew ribbons. The processional begins with the ushers leading, walking in pairs, followed by the junior ushers, then the junior bridesmaids, and the bridesmaids, in pairs. The maid or matron of honor comes next; if there are both, the matron precedes the maid. The flower girl and the ring bearer walk immediately ahead of the bride, who will be on her father's right, holding his arm.

At the altar, the bride moves away from her father to stand at the groom's left side as he steps forward to join her. The father moves left and behind the bride. The best man flanks the groom's right; behind him stands the ring bearer and the ushers in a phalanx to the right. The honor attendant stands on the bride's left, the flower girl behind, the bridesmaids arrayed to the left. After giving his daughter away, the father moves left and back to take his seat.

At double weddings, the two sets of ushers walk ahead of the procession, in pairs, followed by the female attendants of the first bride, then the bride herself on her father's arm. The second retinue of bride's attendants precedes the second bride in similar fashion. If it is a marriage of sisters, the elder bride goes before the younger; the father may deliver her at the altar, then return to escort his younger daughter. He can give both daughters away.

The congregation will, at a sign from the minister, be seated. The couple, with their principal attendants, ring bearer, and flower girl, move up to the altar behind the minister. The bride's bouquet is handed to the maid of honor and the ceremony begins. At a Roman Catholic wedding and Mass, the ceremony takes place after the homily and before the offertory. Without the Mass, the procedure is similar to the Protestant service, although the wording of the liturgy will differ. The best man hands the minister the bride's wedding ring; the maid of honor the groom's. When "man and wife" is pronounced and the couple kiss, the newlyweds, best man, and maid of honor then follow the minister to the table set aside to sign and witness the marriage license. The place in the ceremony for solo readings from the scriptures or from classical literature is decided beforehand. Then the happy couple and the attendants arrange themselves for the recessional, as the music crescendoes.

For a Jewish ceremony, the seating changes according to which tradition the couple belongs to. In Orthodox and Conservative practice, the right is the bride's side, the left the groom's, though at Orthodox weddings men and women are often seated separately. At a Reform service, the left is the bride's side, the right the groom's. The two sets of parents generally remain standing within or just outside of the traditional *chuppah* throughout the ceremony. Or the fathers will remain, and the mothers take their seats after the processional. Bride and groom stand before the Ark, under the *chuppah,* facing the rabbi. Their honor attendants stand with them; ushers and bridesmaids are arranged on each of the outer sides. Since the many procedures are according to local custom and the preferences of the individual rabbi, Jewish services will differ. However, at Orthodox and Conservative weddings all the men assembled must cover their heads, whether with skullcaps, homburgs, or top hats.

In the Jewish processional outside of a temple or synagogue, the rabbi and cantor will lead. Otherwise, they wait as the processional, led by the grandparents in couples, if participating, comes toward them. Or the male ushers lead, in pairs, followed by the best man. Behind him is the groom, flanked by his parents. The bridesmaids come next, in pairs; then the flower girl and ring bearer, and lastly the bride, also with her parents on either side. In the recessional the line begins with the bride and groom, followed by the bride's parents, the groom's parents, the maid or matron of honor with the best man, and the bridesmaids, each on the arm of an usher.

Music shapes and gives richness to each segment of the ceremony, of which it is a vital part. The selections must be arranged with the music director or organist or cantor. The repertory of classical and religious music suitable for a wedding is long and often very familiar, but no less joyous for that. Wagner's "Bridal Chorus" from *Lohengrin* ("Here Comes the Bride") for the processional and the "Wedding March" from Mendelssohn's *A Midsummer Night's Dream* for the recessional are standard. The religious establishment may allow you to bring in musicians to supplement the organ, or to play taped music. Popular tunes as well can be aired at weddings, but you will be losing something. There is a spirituality, a majesty, an exuberance in great passages from the classical repertoire that an everyday romantic tune cannot hope to match. However, a song that means something special to you both may be included, if desired.

Your musical choices will begin with half an hour of prelude music; then perhaps a solo or choral piece while the two mothers are being seated; the processional music; the songs or hymns and, lastly and magnificently, the recessional music. You can think of it in terms of imagery: a quiet brook, then a river and, finally, a waterfall. If you don't know what you want, consult the local library; discuss the question with your church or synagogue; listen to classical music on the radio, or ask a musically knowledgeable friend. All can help you to put together something magical.

THE WEDDING RING(S)

The wedding ring goes back to pharaonic Egypt, and has been fashioned from materials as diverse as bulrushes and iron. In Shakespeare's time it became the vogue to inscribe gold wedding rings with mottoes or poesies. Gemologist, author, and former Tiffany vice president George F. Kunz recounted these cautionary words discovered in a seventeenth-century wedding ring: "Love him who gave thee this ring of gold/'Tis he must kiss thee when thou art old."[*]

When a modern couple steps through a fine jeweler's door to find the ring or rings to bind their vows, they will encounter many kinds of wedding bands, both plain and fancy. Most will choose the traditional plain or mill-grain edge 18-karat gold band, and will have each other's initials engraved inside. The practice of exchanging betrothal rings is on the increase. Men rarely select platinum, so double rings are always of gold.

A karat is the unit of weight which expresses the proportion of gold to an alloy—i.e.: 18-karat gold is 75 percent fine gold. The alloy may be silver, which gives a green hue; copper, which gives a red hue, or nickel and zinc, which gives a white hue. The softest is 24-karat gold and is not suitable for wedding bands; 14-karat gold is the hardest-wearing. The 18-karat gold used for wedding

[*] George F. Kunz, *Rings for the Finger* (first published 1917; reprinted New York: Dover Publications, 1973).

rings is more vibrant in color than 14-karat gold. Platinum is a harder metal than gold.

Some brides forgo an engagement ring in order to put the money to other uses, then desire something more romantic for their wedding rings—perhaps a circle glittering with stones. They can luxuriate in a band ring of 18-karat gold, set with all diamonds or alternating diamonds with colored stones, in complete or half circles.

PHOTOGRAPHY AND VIDEO

No great production is staged without a professional photographer on hand to record it. Relatives' or friends' cameras can capture some lively moments at your wedding, but the experienced eye of a good photographer will do much more. An album of high-quality color photographs, close-ups, vignettes, candid shots, becomes your most treasured, sometimes the only visual record of the event. Videotapes are another, newer method of encapsulating the day.

An excellent photographer is always busy, so you must book his or her services well in advance. Word of mouth is still the best way to find one, or you might have attended a party where the skill of the photographer impressed you. Make an appointment with several studios, and go through their portfolios or sample wedding albums.

Every wedding is different, yet there is a definite routine which ensures that no cardinal moment or person of importance is overlooked. Generally the photographer arrives at the home of the bride about one and a half hours before the service to take the formal portraits of the bride, her attendants, and her close family. At Jewish ceremonies the photographer is usually allowed to record the rehearsal which, at nine out of ten Jewish weddings, takes place at the ceremony's location half an hour before the service itself. Christian churches have house rules regarding photography, so the couple must check first and convey the information to the photographer.

At the reception the photographer captures the big moments: the receiving line, the toasts, the cake cutting, and the going away as well as the dining and dancing. When an agreement between you and the photographer is reached, a professional contract is drawn up which specifies the day, time, and all the locations, the number of albums required, delivery date, and an estimated cost. Photography is in color throughout, and for indoors the cameraman should work with a flash lamp on his own camera, and another carried by an assistant. Three wedding albums—for bride and groom and each set of parents—is the standard order at an estimated $1,000 to $1,500 all-inclusive cost. Extra prints add to this, of course.

Video Sound

The best video sound professionals are found, again, by word of mouth. Ask a photography studio you trust for a recommendation, then interview more than one, and view a demonstration tape before you decide. A typical video, finished and edited, lasts one and one half hours, for which a cameraman and his assistant will spend up to two hours at the wedding. You can choose to have an unedited version for a little less.

Andy Wander, president of Occasional Video of New York, advises that: "No one would want to watch five hours of an unedited tape of a wedding. So plan your coverage for the important moments." How intrusive is videotaping depends on how lavish you want the end result. At a small wedding, one cameraman with a light on his camera can obtain superb pictures and sound. For outdoor tent weddings, the cameraman will use the available daylight. Movie-theater quality is an ambitious undertaking, with big crew, multiple cameras and banks of lights.

The contractual agreement makes clear when the cameraman and crew member should be present, and whether you want the tape edited. An average one-and-one-half-hour video, unedited, costs about $750. The tape will be ready from two weeks to two months after the wedding, depending upon length and how much editing is involved.

THE REHEARSAL

The rehearsal takes place a day or two before the wedding, and every member involved attends. The officiating minister, his assistants, the organist, cantor, or choir, and any extra musicians or additional readers should be there also. If you have hired a bridal consultant, you might wish her to be present to offer advice.

Since the ceremony differs greatly among the religious denominations, the officiator directs proceedings, as he or she is familiar with the ritual. The rehearsal is not a complete run-through of the service, but touches upon the main points to ensure that bride and groom know their responses, and to give everyone an opportunity to practice their moves. The Christian church rehearsal usually takes place in the early evening or late afternoon on the day before the wedding. The religious officials appreciate punctuality, and serious attention from all the participants. The Jewish wedding rehearsal may be conducted on the wedding day, just prior to the ceremony.

The Rehearsal Dinner

Whether held at home or in a restaurant, the dinner which follows the rehearsal is an event enjoyed by all. Traditionally thrown by the groom's parents, although it can be given by any relative, it provides the wedding party and families time to relax and become better acquainted. It is thoughtful to invite out-of-town guests as well, if there is no other time to entertain them before the wedding. The toasts, kept brief at the wedding reception, can be indulged in here.

Whoever is the host can set the style of the event to further friendly relationships. Should the groom's parents give the dinner, they might select food which illuminates their background if it differs from that of the bride's family. Whatever the form, the rehearsal dinner is an ideal time for the bride and groom to give the attendants their gifts, if they have not already done so. In some communities it is the custom for best man and ushers to join in purchasing a special keepsake gift from them to the bride and groom. Presented on the eve of the wedding, it is often a sterling silver tray, covered box or similar item, with their signatures engraved across it.

THE WEDDING BREAKFAST

On the wedding morning, while the bride is occupied in having a facial or getting her hair and makeup done, a nice gesture from a family member or neighbor is to hold a wedding breakfast for the out-of-town guests. It fills the waiting hours in a convivial manner and allows yet another affectionate relative or friend a chance to add their own golden moment to the day.

Since the next meal will be many hours off, the breakfast can be hearty: traditional eggs, bacon, and sausages with homemade pancakes, biscuits, or popovers; or the host can show off special home-baked breads. Serve exotic fruit juices, such as guava or papaya, or have a generous fresh fruit salad available. Some guests may appreciate mimosas—champagne and fresh orange juice—as the only way to start a festive day right.

THE RECEPTION

Location

The guests' cars are arriving from the ceremony in droves. Women, lovely in long dresses, hand in hand with their handsome men, are drifting across green lawns to the light-wreathed tent. The young bride, now bareheaded if she chooses, yet a vision in white, is being showered with love and congratulations. People hug, glasses tinkle, waiters progress. That is the romance of it—a priceless moment, an extravaganza, the parents' last hurrah for their just-married daughter.

It happens at all traditional weddings across the country—the emotion and the gaiety, the poignancy and the joy when, to quote an old cliché, a family loses a daughter and gains a son. Where to hold the reception, if it is in a different place from the ceremony, is the next most soul-searched question. More than ever, people with houses and gardens large enough are choosing a catered affair at home. A wedding breakfast or reception at a hotel or restaurant strikes many people as too impersonal. However, an inventive stylist, given carte blanche to create a fantasy, can transform a hired space into pure theater—such as the forest of tall trees hung with a thousand orchids, and the huge billowing net with stuffed white doves "flying" across it which delighted Texas high society at a recent wedding in a Dallas hotel.

People make the decision about the reception based on their budget, their resources, the time of day, and the weddings they themselves have attended and enjoyed. Morning weddings are followed by a wedding "breakfast," actually a lunch. Parents and close friends may gather in the evening, after the newlyweds have departed, for a more intimate dinner. Late afternoon weddings are followed by a reception, which can take the form of an immense cocktail party where hors d'oeuvres and finger foods are served; or a buffet or seated dinner with dancing, which goes on into the late evening.

For a reception outdoors, your guests may need shelter from the hot sun at daytime or from moisture-laden coolness in the evening. A party tent is the classic solution, and white the most favored color for a wedding, although stripes and solid colors add their own aesthetics. You can hire the tent or tents from a tent company, which also supplies the tables and chairs. Every expert agrees that round tables seating ten for a sit-down dinner are the most successful configuration. At tables this size people become friendlier because relaxed; traffic flow is better and it is easier for the waiters to serve. You will need to hire long tables for buffet food and for setting up bars. The tent people will want to examine and measure the site weeks beforehand; then, two or three days before the wedding, they will reappear to set up the tent and bring other basic equipment.

You have thought of the florist, caterer, and photographer, but may have forgotten the all-important lighting expert. Time and energy spent on decorating the setting can be wasted without good lighting, subtly diffused to cast a soft glow over all. And barmen and waiters need adequately lit serving stations. Some of the professionals you hire—the florist or the caterer—work with lighting designers. Many will insist on bringing them in to illuminate the setting correctly.

Thomas Baumgarten, Tiffany's Manager of Special Events, says: "People will turn their homes and gardens into one big festive environment. I have seen them cover two football fields with wood planking, topped by massive tents, so that they can entertain three hundred and fifty to four hundred people in their own backyard. The swimming pool is always covered; it's just the size for a dance floor."

With all the big city resources at hand, an apartment in town can be transformed into a wedding chapel, then become an elegant setting for a dinner reception for twenty or thirty guests afterward. Whatever the location, it is the backdrop for a most glorious day in the families' lives.

Decorating the Reception

The wedding reception decorations not only create a beautiful ambience for celebration, but express the individual tastes and interests of the bride and groom. Flowers and greenery will play their part, but decorative objects can be brought into play—swagged fabric, ribbons, strings of tiny lights or balloons. The creative people you hire are often concerned with how they can make this wedding different. They can, if you are prepared to participate, to open avenues for debate and listen to their suggestions.

As designer John Funt says, "At the ceremony, everything can be classic, but there is no reason why the reception decoration can't be quite daring and original. Even in the most traditional of circumstances, a sense of humor and adventure is very nice." The time of year can be fully utilized, stirring instincts related to times long past when life was lived to the rhythm of the seasons. In this, Funt finds his muse: "I believe in following the seasons at any party or reception I decorate. In June, flowers are of course at their best, but in autumn, mounds of glowing fruit and things brought in from the field are wonderful. A winter garden looks very romantic for a winter wedding; or you can achieve crystalline effects with thin silver fabric, warmed by articles finished in gold, even gold paper with piles of candied fruits and sugared almonds. You have to rely less on flowers for effect."

Seasonal and regional foods served at a reception can be a key element affecting the decoration. New York caterer Susan Holland comments, "I have both cooked and decorated weddings. Once, when we were serving Southwestern food, I used my own collection of big old silver candlesticks

Michel's at the Colony Surf Hotel on Waikiki Beach has been called the most romantic restaurant in the world.

The tables set for an evening wedding reception, Michel's is ablaze with thousands of the small pastel-colored orchids that proliferate on Hawaii, held in Tiffany vermeil pitchers.

Tiffany Private Stock "Strasbourg" platters hold Colony Surf's Executive Chef Gordon Hopkins's buffet supper of canapés of roast duckling slivers with sauce bigarade, cucumber slices with smoked salmon, shrimp, horseradish cream, and black caviar served alongside a platter of lobster and snow crab claws.

The embroidered linens are from Léron.

on bare pine tables, surrounded by hordes of cactuses in little pots. Romantic does not always have to be the English country look."

The setting, especially the impersonal public rooms of a hotel or similar space, can be made memorable when bride and groom realize that tradition need not be ironclad. Not everything has to be color-coordinated with the bridesmaids' dresses (as standard etiquette is apt to recommend). Make a statement; put some of your own possessions around: sets of napkins, flower containers, candy dishes, candle holders.

Nonetheless, an acre of ballroom or tent interior can be daunting. Florist Marlo Phillips advises, "Someone has to be the aesthetic guide, or the whole thing is going to look like alphabet soup. When I get involved, I check up on the dress, food, cake; where the bars will be; where the traffic areas; everything. It's like landscaping." Some practicalities to note are: round dining tables together in great quantity need cloths to the floor, to eliminate a sea of table legs. In a large space, the sheer yardage of tablecloth can be considerable—the first thing the eye takes in. So ensure that fabric color and decoration harmonize with the environment. Table centerpieces shouldn't block the view, as there are toasts to participate in and people to watch.

If the reception space is a big rectangle, traditional long tables will achieve an entirely different effect. They can be dressed formally with starched white cloths and napkins, massed blooms in silver bowls, patterned china, good flatware and crystal. Or more casually with an idea from New York floral designer Valorie Hart: "If the bride and groom are at a long table, to make it important I create a 'tablescape.' A great mass of dried flowers, some potpourri and loose blooms are strewn along the center length. I ask the bride for some personal objects and memorabilia; put the wedding invitation in a silver frame and include these things as well. Sometimes the bridesmaids add their bouquets. It is very effective—almost medieval."

The wedding cake should receive star treatment also. Have it set up in splendor and carefully lit. For the cake-cutting ceremony, it can be surrounded by an attractive dessert course to complete the picture for the photographer.

Receiving Line

Members of the wedding party are expected to form the traditional receiving line at the reception entrance, to greet guests arriving from the ceremony. It gives everyone a chance to become introduced and to offer congratulations. At a small, intimate wedding you may dispense with a line, but at a large wedding it is vital. The space involved must be thought out in advance. Arriving guests need somewhere to leave their coats, somewhere to collect together. The offer of a glass of champagne as people wait to go through the line is much appreciated, but guests must relinquish their glasses before being received.

The receiving line is assembled as follows:

mother of the bride

mother of the groom

bride

groom

maid or matron of honor

bridesmaids

If the fathers are not too busy circulating, they may stand in line:

mother of the bride

father of the groom

mother of the groom

father of the bride

and so on.

The best man and ushers do not stand in the receiving line, and bridesmaids can forgo the pleasure if it is too lengthy. If the parents are divorced, usually only the natural mother stands in line. If a stepparent is hosting the party, he or she will stand in the receiving line. The wedding party members introduce the guest to the next person on line. It is not usual to wear gloves when receiving or being received.

Seating

If the reception is a buffet, or a seated luncheon or dinner with waiter service, you need place cards and a firm seating plan. The scheme for the main tables is based, once again, on tradition. At the bride and groom's table, which is waited upon even if it is a buffet, sit the maid or matron of honor to the groom's left; the best man to the bride's right. Their spouses or companions may be invited to sit at the table, along with senior bridesmaids and their escorts. At the parents' table sit the mothers and fathers of bride and groom, the grandparents, godparents, and the person who performed the ceremony along with his or her spouse. The bride's mother takes the central position, with the father of the groom on her right; the father of the bride sits with the groom's mother on his right. Gentleman and lady alternate from there. Your other attendants and their escorts may be at a table together, or seated all about. Flower girl, ring bearer, and junior attendants will be happier seated with their parents. Good sense will help to put together tables of guests who will find each other stimulating and enjoyable.

The Toasts

The best man proposes the first toast to the bride and groom, when everyone is either assembled or has been seated and the champagne poured. Everyone except bride and groom stands. Then the groom rises and toasts his bride and new in-laws. The bride may propose a toast of her own, then the parents, and so on in a spontaneous way throughout the meal. The best man reads the telegrams at suitable moments, after the first toasts and perhaps during the salad course.

CATERING AND MENUS

Americans are used to exciting food, the blending of cuisines national and international. At a wedding, the feast is central to the celebration and expectations are high. The table settings, the menu, the anxiety about getting it right—is when most families need help. America's topflight professional caterers are kept busy year-round by the demand for their services.

The names of reputable caterers are passed by word of mouth. Some are so fashionable that you have to be grateful when they agree to take you on. Like New York's Glorious Food, who will create what they describe as "a total dining experience." This means that they will bring in everything but the tent and the kitchen stove. Sean Driscoll, owner of Glorious Food, says: "Almost nobody calls us just to arrive with the food anymore. At a wedding, emotions are running high. Our advice for a big reception is to have everybody involved channel into one experienced person: a party planner, the floral designer, or one of us."

The sensible place for the first meeting between caterer and client is at the site, whether country or city, a good six months prior to the wedding. The caterer assesses the kitchen's potential, the work and dining areas, and the family's tastes. The location and time of day will often dictate the kind of food it is best to serve. Most caterers prefer the meeting to be with the bride as well as with her mother, to get a better idea of likes and dislikes.

"At a wedding, nobody wants to be too experimental with the food," Driscoll says. "A formal affair calls for a classic entrée, like stuffed loin of veal, breast of capon, or fillet of beef with a truffle sauce. If the father of the bride is footing the bill, he wants the fare to appear substantial. No one should go away hungry. We will serve a fish course, the main course, salad, and dessert with the wedding cake. We hope the entire meal will be memorable, but something innovative will be present in at least one of the courses, just to surprise people." Driscoll's idea is for everyone to have a glorious time. His favorite anecdote recalls the anxious mother who, two or three days before the wedding, telephoned to enquire whether the pea-and-mint soup planned might create a color clash with the green of the bridesmaids' Adolfo-designed dresses: "That was a tough one!"

The caterer you employ is expected to hold one or two tasting sessions for you, and advise you about the china, crystal, flatware, serving platters, and ice buckets required for the day and to supply or hire them. The charges are based on a packaged cost per head, which should include all drinks, rental fees, and any other service the caterer is providing. Add 15 to 25 percent for tax and gratuities.

The standard staffing for a serious, seated four-course dinner is two and a half waiters per table of ten for good service. This allows enough staff to deal with cocktails and clearing. On the day of the reception, one third of the caterer's staff—the chefs, captains and some of the waiters—will arrive up to two or three hours beforehand to set up. When the remainder arrive, an hour is spent explaining the menu, and giving directions about serving the wines.

To repeat, what is served is a reflection of the kind of wedding reception you want. Here are some menu ideas for educated palates, provided by several outstanding caterers:

Ida Mae's Cakes of Jacksboro, Texas, for over forty years has been creating extravagant wedding cakes of legendary originality and intricacy.

This five-foot-tall bride's cake designed by owner Becky Sikes Crump in the form of a "vase" bursting with edible icing flowers confirms founder Ida Mae Stark's dictum: "There has never been a recession with wedding cakes." "Some," says Becky Crump, "cost more than a down payment on a house and some are bigger than cars."

A Tiffany "English King" cake knife tied with multicolored ribbons waits for the bride to cut this masterpiece of American folk art.

From Glorious Food, New York

Wedding Luncheon

1st course	Cold cucumber soup with yogurt, sour cream, and caviar
2nd course	Breast of capon with morel mousse and morel sauce
	Sautéed spinach
	Spaetzle
Dessert	Wedding cake
	Raspberries, blueberries, and strawberries, with fresh raspberry sauce
	Coffee / Chocolate truffles

Wedding Dinner

1st course	Salad of mâche with lobster, scallops, and caviar
	Lemon caviar mousseline
2nd course	Medallions of veal with black truffle sauce
	Glazed vegetables
	Potato tart
Dessert	Wedding cake
	Pomegranate ice cream in pomegranate shell
	Coffee / Chocolate truffles

From Susan Holland, New York

Outdoor Summer Wedding Buffet

1st course	Warm Parmesan leaves with wild mushroom duxelles
	Shrimp beignets
	Smoked chicken with ginger chutney sauce
	Indonesian beef saté
2nd course	Grilled half baby chickens with honeycup mustard or spicy salsa and corn relishes
	Misto mare (mixed seafood) with langoustines and mussels in shallots and fresh herbs
	White-truffle pasta with fresh baby artichokes, fennel, and roasted peppers

Salad rustica with field greens, radicchio, lola rosa, baked ricotta, and Moroccan olives

French and Italian farm breads, biscotti and focaccia, served with Normandy butter

Dessert   Wedding cake

Fresh cherries and chocolates

Coffee / Herbal teas

From Andrea Whitefield's Food Company, Dallas

Wedding Luncheon

1st course   Spanish red shrimp with rémoulade sauce

2nd course   Thai chicken flavored with lemon grass, fresh mint, and basil, on a bed of shredded red cabbage and lettuce

Julienne of jicama and carrots with lime juice

Rice salad with peas, red sweet peppers, scallions, hazelnuts, and mint

Sage- or rosemary-scented bread

Dessert   Wedding cake: a homemade rich, dense, three-layer chocolate cake, served with homemade cinnamon ice cream

Coffee / Fine teas

From Caroly Pettyjohn's Party Service Inc., Dallas

Wedding Dinner

1st course   Fried quail and fried okra

Biscuits

2nd course   Beef tenderloin stuffed with lobster and mushrooms

Brown rice with almonds and onions

Baked summer squash

Sweet and sour garden salad with avocado and oranges

Dessert   Wedding cake: a spiced Louisiana pecan cake, served with homemade vanilla ice cream

Coffee

From Fred Wertheim Experience, San Francisco
  Wedding Reception/Dinner
  Hors d'oeuvres   Crisped new potato skins filled with sour cream and black caviar
                   Dungeness crab legs in endive leaves
                   Beignets of artichoke hearts on a skewer, with Béarnaise sauce
                   Chinese snow peas, stuffed with herbed creamed cheese and watercress
  Dinner
  1st course   Giant ravioli filled with wild mushrooms, served with two sauces: red
                     pepper and essence of wild mushrooms
  2nd course   California quail, herbed and grilled, with wild rice pancakes
                   Mélange of baby vegetables
                   Salad of baby lettuces garnished with roasted walnuts and walnut oil
                     dressing
                   Goat cheese with homemade sourdough melbas
  Dessert   Wedding cake
                   Giant stem strawberries with zabaglione sauce
                   Coffee

From R. C. Wilford Catering, New York
  June Wedding Dinner
  1st course   Cold medallions of Maine lobster tail with diced cucumber and kiwi-
                     pear vinaigrette
  2nd course   Roast loin of veal with apricot and shallot stuffing, served with
                     Madeira sauce
                   Baby red beets
                   Julienne of early summer squash
                   Lyonnaise potatoes
                   Salad of mâche, endive, and Boston lettuce with warm hazelnut oil
                     vinaigrette and domestic chèvres
  Dessert   Wedding cake
                   White chocolate mousse with fresh raspberry sauce and dark chocolate
                     langue-de-chats
                   Coffee

Wines

To serve a crowd, you will want light, palatable, not-too-expensive wines to accompany the food. Your caterer or local wine merchant can give you good advice. Fruity California whites go well with a variety of dishes: try the Chardonnays, Gewürztraminers, Sauvignon Blancs, or a Muscadet from France. Among the reds, French Beaujolais nouveau (after late November) is fresh, delicious, and a conversation piece; Beaujolais types to consider are Fleurie, Chiroubles and, better still, Moulin-à-Vent. Some *petit château* French Bordeaux wines are excellent when still fairly young: research among the St. Emilions. For sparkle, serve California Blanc-de-Blancs or Blanc-de-Noirs or French *vins mousseux* from the Loire Valley, or one of the useful Spanish cava sparkling wines.

The Wedding Cake

The artistry, the control, the know-how and the timing involved in producing the wedding cake are such that its makers and decorators are really a breed apart. Their fantastic confections are superb: they embody ritual, are dazzlingly picturesque, and you can eat them.

The Romans made a nuptial cake of barley flour, water, and salt to crumble over the bride's head and bless her with fertility. The Elizabethans prepared small spiced currant cakes which, by the reign of Charles II, had evolved into a large fruitcake, covered with sugar icing. As the wedding feast grew ever larger, so did the bridecake, as it was called. By the Victorian age, the wedding cake was an architectural triumph in white sugar: a tiered, niched, pilastered, swagged, domed, beflowered and beribboned edifice replete with bells, cherubs, and coats of arms. Today people favor two or three tiers, covered with flowers built from sugar dough which are miracles of realism, or with living blooms pushed into soft frosting at the penultimate moment before the cake is displayed.

Most American towns have at least one well-respected baker for wedding and special occasion cakes. Bigger cities boast several, each with their own particular style. Sylvia Weinstock, New York's doyenne of wedding cakes, recalls she was inspired by the memory of "those wonderful, romantic-looking wedding cakes that Schrafft's used to make over twenty years ago." Weinstock's cakes revive that feeling, garlanded as they are with extraordinary colored flowers made with a mixture of sugar, water, and gelatin, hand-painted with vegetable dyes. "I meet with the bride," Weinstock says, "to discuss the flowers she is planning to have on the tables, so that I can incorporate some of the same blooms on her cake. I love to create a basket weave with mixed English country

*W*hile peacocks strut by two koa rocking chairs to inspect a mass of red bananas and golden coconuts, a round antique koa wood table holds Mauna Lani chef Peter Merriman's traditional flower-decked Hawaiian bride's cake.

A Tiffany "Laurelton Hall" champagne flute is tied with a gardenia and ti-leaf bow to toast the bride; banded with a fresh flower haku lei, a straw bridesmaid's hat rests on the back of a chair.

The traditional Hawaiian planter's cottage stands in the gardens of the Mauna Lani Bay Hotel.

*T*he groom's cake was originally an American Southern tradition. World-celebrated Jacksboro, Texas, bakery, Ida Mae's Cakes, demonstrates mixed theatricality and whimsy by this "Della Robbia" groom's cake whose marzipan fruits wreathe a seventeenth-century Italian angel.

Ida Mae's suggests a German chocolate cake with chocolate icing for the groom, or carrot, spice, red devil's food, or white chocolate cake as alternatives.

flowers like roses, sweet peas, and tulips. Or a cake dripping with purple wisteria, something I did recently for an 1890s-theme wedding."

Ninety-eight percent of a cake's decoration is edible. The cake base may be a vanilla-flavored pound cake, or a white sponge, nut torte, chocolate, carrot, or cheesecake. In the South, as in Europe, they prefer a fruitcake, which elsewhere in the country is a groom's cake, if there is one.

A very famous cake lady is the now semi-retired Ida Mae Stark of Jacksboro, Texas. Ida Mae's fairy-tale cakes were what you ordered down big country way. The company, owned and run by Becky Sikes Crump, continues her tradition. Ida Mae's signature "fluties," a narrow, bell-like flower shape, expands from tier to tier and, like a towering sculpture, everything is held together with hidden steel supports. An Ida Mae cake to serve seventy-five people averages 22 inches in diameter and 22 inches in height. But this being Texas, it is sometimes five-tiered, standing six feet high and serving 1,200 people.

Not everyone wants a flowery, rococo cake—but most do. If your taste is for neoclassical, or Art Deco, or tailored, with pulled sugar bows (from Maurice Bonté, New York), there is a master cakemaker who can create it for you. Talk to friends, look through books and magazines, or go to the best baker you know. Make an appointment, if necessary, and you will be shown a lavish portfolio of wedding cake styles. You can combine the trimming of one with the shape of another, if you wish. They are custom-made, so anything is possible. The better the quality and more imaginative the cake, the higher the price. Many-tiered cakes serving a few hundred people can run into several thousand dollars. "People will pay anything, if they want the cake," says Becky Crump. To which Mrs. Burbidge of Boston would add, "Brides feel it is the next most important thing at the wedding after themselves."

Cile Bellefleur Burbidge—teacher, lecturer, author of a book on cake decorating—is today a classicist in the field. She dislikes incorporating butter-cream fillings in case the cake "moves" during transportation and breaks the frosting. For Mrs. Burbidge, a well-flavored pound cake has the qualities of support she seeks, but she will make carrot and chocolate bases. She does all the decoration herself, preferring to work on one to three tiers. She is a legend in the Boston area for the breathtaking perfection of her filigree and trellis patterns, covered with delicate flowers and sprays. "Brides are marrying a few years older nowadays, so they are more mature," she observes. "They want an elegant, feminine cake."

At the reception, the cake is set at the center of a buffet table, or upon a cloth-draped table of its own. If spotlit, be sure the lamp is not so hot as to affect the cake. The cake cutting is a regal moment, likely to dissolve into hilarity as bride and groom wrestle to extricate the first slice which they are expected to feed to each other. A waiter completes the slicing and the pieces are generally offered along with a dessert: a chocolate or raspberry mousse, for example, fruit sorbets, or homemade ice cream.

The Groom's Cake

The dark European fruitcake evolved into the groom's cake in America many decades ago. Traditionally it is cut, wrapped, placed in tiny cake boxes, and distributed to the guests for good luck. This time-consuming effort and cost has rendered the practice unrealistic. A rich chocolate cake, to be shared with their first guests when the couple return from their honeymoon, is now more usual.

Music and Dancing

Music at your reception is the mood enhancer *sans pareil,* and live musicians are much more fun than cassette tapes. You can hire a diversity of musical talent, from a string trio to a jazz combo to a twenty-three-piece dance orchestra. Strolling musicians add color to a seated dinner; a small group will create a low-key background of pleasant sound. A professional DJ, who programs several hours of taped music from classical to rock—but usually rock—is another direction to take. This is useful if you want to set aside an area for the younger crowd to enjoy, without hiring a separate rock group.

For dancing you need tempo and melodies old and new to please everybody. There are the famous society dance orchestras of Lester Lanin or Peter Duchin, who work from coast to coast at all manner of private functions. There are hundreds of experienced musicians available as well. Ask friends; check the yellow pages, your college music department, or the local musicians' union.

The first ten presidents of the United States frequented the dinner table of Berkeley Plantation, the ancestral home of the Harrison family, built in 1726, and birthplace of two presidents, Benjamin Harrison and William Henry Harrison.

Here the current owners, Mr. and Mrs. Malcolm Jamieson, have set this most historic dining room for a traditional Southern wedding reception which will include a Smithfield ham, punch, and plenty of sweets in addition to the three-tiered wedding

cake which will be cut with a Tiffany "English King" cake knife tied with white ribbons and one pink garden rosebud.

The point de Venise lace tablecloth was a wedding present to the Jamiesons in 1937.

The available space and the type of reception you are planning will be key factors, of course. Listen to the band of your choice play at least once, either at an audition or wherever they may be working. A dance band performs Gershwin and Cole Porter standards, show tunes, current hits, waltzes, Latin numbers, and so forth. The first dance of the evening is always the bride and groom's, so request your favorite song, with several of the families' well-loved tunes to follow. Traditionally, the bride's father either cuts in or takes the second dance with his daughter, while the groom dances with his mother. The groom's father will move onto the floor with the bride's mother and after a round or two the floor is open for the guests.

Bandleader Lester Lanin, who started his career in 1945, introduced up-tempo, nonstop dance music to America. His many albums have titles like: *Twisting in High Society,* and *Narrowing the Generation Gap.* He says, "Music is an integral part of a wedding reception. It should be lively, fast-paced, bright and upbeat. A whole evening of, say, Polish, Greek, Italian, Jewish or society music would be a crime. The program should be like a well-mixed cocktail."

Tossing the Bouquet and Garter

After the cake cutting and some dancing, it is time for bride and groom to leave the reception to change clothes and depart on their honeymoon. This is the moment to toss your bouquet to the unmarried bridesmaids and your garter to the unattached ushers. Word is passed around, and the two groups are expected to assemble. Then the bride, with merry ceremony and her back turned if she wishes, throws the bouquet to the waiting ladies. Superstition decrees, of course, that whoever catches it will be the next to marry.

As for the garter, if it were Shakespeare's bawdier times all the young men would be stripping the bride of her garters, ribbons, and laces. Today the groom can more gracefully slip it off and toss it to the waiting men. The same married luck will befall whoever captures it.

Going Away

The day is not yet over. You have been "helped" into your travel clothes by emotional parents and attendants, and are about to receive the customary send-off. It makes no difference whether you are merely going a few paces to the beach house, or a block or two to a good hotel; "going away" is the day's last big public moment. So your outfit should be sensational; you can change into those hiking boots and blue jeans later. You will both be showered with rice, birdseed, paper rose petals, or confetti. Old shoes (for good fortune in travel and in life) are tied to your conveyance—for that is the tradition and everybody loves it.

The best man's final tasks are to see that travel documents, passports, luggage, and whatever else you will need goes with you. He arranges for the men's formal wear to be returned to the rental company as soon as possible. Your maid or matron of honor will take your dress to a custom cleaners and have it carefully wrapped and stored for you. After which, it is goodbye to the old life and on with the new.

HER PERSONAL TROUSSEAU AND GOING-AWAY CLOTHES

You are off at last on the long-awaited honeymoon, elated in your smart new clothes and picking confetti out of your husband's hair. Your personal trousseau, every woman's most treasured and planned-for wardrobe, is packed in your squeaky-new luggage. Another important rite of passage is taking place, one that links you to all the brides from centuries past.

Since medieval days, the young bride's trousseau has consisted of new under and outer garments, as well as articles for her household. The Victorian trousseau contained "a dozen of everything," and took months to assemble. From her engrossing book *And the Bride Wore . . . ,*[*] British writer Ann Monsarrat relays a young English socialite's description of her trousseau in 1920. Besides copious amounts of underclothes, there were: "A dozen pairs of evening and day shoes . . . two evening dresses suited to winter . . . two tea gowns . . . three day dresses and three afternoon dresses . . . three tweed suits and a travelling coat, with matching hats and jerseys and shirts. My going-away dress was of pale blue marocaine, with a skirt cut into petals, topped by a black velvet coat with a grey fox collar, and a grey cap trimmed with ospreys." This was a bright young thing who knew how to dress for an exit.

Your trousseau is of course a matter of your personal style and available budget, but most brides relish glamorous sleeping attire and lingerie. Confections of silk and satin, lavished with lace, are available. The French, influential as ever, have led the way to a lingerie renaissance with corselets, bustiers, suspender belts, and thigh-high stockings—underpinnings in keeping with the shapelier silhouettes of fashion. At fine stores and boutiques, you will find the most luxurious lingerie, often

---

[*] Ann Monsarrat, *And the Bride Wore . . .* (New York: Dodd, Mead & Company, 1974).

with hand-finished detail, by better European makers like: Aubade, Pascale Madonna, Gemma and Scandale, all of France; or Sabbia and Malizia Rosa of Italy. Some American manufacturers have responded with special lines of romantic trousseau items, and fancier underthings for every day. This is your moment to splurge.

American lingerie designer Carole Hochman, who creates for both Christian Dior and for her own label, believes a bride "wants everything new. That is how she views the marriage—as starting from scratch." Hochman often adapts her styles from antique lingerie in her own collection. Her conviction is that "Every woman looks better in beautiful lingerie, no matter how fabulous her body is. Lingerie should be worn like jewelry: to enhance what is already there. It is an important part of what being a bride, being female, is all about." Hochman's special bridal trousseau line for Christian Dior is called "Le Connaisseur," and is available, on order, at better department stores.

Couture-designed ready-to-wear lingerie has become part of seasonal collections by top designers, such as Giorgio Armani, Calvin Klein, Fernando Sanchez, and Koos Van Den Akker. Fernando Sanchez is a Spanish-born couturier whose taste and style have been influential in America. Sanchez designs what he calls "Clothes for Private Lives"—imaginative leisurewear that is ideally suited to young and sophisticated lifestyles. His peignoir sets are extravaganzas of flowing silk and lace; pajamas for men have tops matched to cuffed shorts, and he makes kimono-type reversible robes for both sexes in luscious sherbet colors. He comments, "People strive for an attractive appearance outside the home, so the same attitude should carry into one's private life. One isn't always alone: there are husbands, lovers, children, friends, houseguests. Private life is multidimensional: when the obligations of the working day are over, it begins."

Since love and marriage guarantee the bride an enraptured audience of one, she can give her imagination free rein. A fine satin-and-lace peignoir set, without which no trousseau is complete, if couture-designed will run between $800 and $900, on order from specialized boutiques. An investment of about $2,500 on your lingerie and sleeping wardrobe is not unreasonable.

In the Middle Ages people slept entirely nude, thus the *trousse* or bundle the bride brought with her to her new abode had a different emphasis—that is, upon outer garments, household linens, pots and pans. Back then, women wore layer upon layer of clothes—just as we slaves to fashion do today. The modern bride knows that clothes define personality, so her personal trousseau is a wardrobe that counts. Are you, in fact, the wrap and layer type? Does red and black do for you what it does for Paloma Picasso? Think about style, and what your working and social life as a new

*L*ingerie designer Carole Hochman believes the bridal trousseau should include four or five nightgowns, a robe to throw on when breakfast arrives at the honeymoon hotel, long-sleeved satin pajamas for glamorous evenings at home, as well as short camisoles and teddies. Shown here in Carole Hochman's Manhattan bedroom designed by Rubén de Saavedra is a selection of silks and satins from her special bridal trousseau line.

wife will be. Choose clothes for changes of mood: soft and dreamy for evening, sharp for daytime, funky for fun. If your honeymoon is a Kenya safari, you won't need a sable. Plan honeymoon clothes and a good wardrobe to return home to—something to see you through two seasons. Any classic styles among your present clothes can be spruced up with different belts, scarves, and costume jewelry, so don't discard them all.

If your shopping time is too rushed, or you need advice, enlist the services of a personal shopper at your favorite department store. They are there to help you with everything you will need.

Consider a range of printed cotton travel luggage to hold makeup and accessories—those plasticized quilted holders in coordinated patterns of flowers, polka dots, or stripes. You can buy smart and useful traveling makeup bags, stocking and shoe holders, jewelry roll, lingerie holder, slippers, and even a dog carrier. Finally, because your trousseau will have cost many hundreds of dollars, don't forget to take out travel insurance.

HIS GOING-AWAY CLOTHES

Men long held to conservative traditions in dress. The Edwardian dandy, the 1920s sophisticate, and the long-haired hippie of the 1960s were incidental to the conservative male viewpoint. However, just put the average young man into a uniform and see how he is transformed. Movies, the media, and world-famous couturiers have done much to bring about a change in men's clothes. The new male responds to fashion with enthusiasm; his clothes are more individually flattering, more relaxed, more imaginative.

The groom's going-away clothes can create as much interest in terms of style as the bride's. In the United States today, men have an enormous range of international designer fashion from which to choose. American designers like Bijan, Bill Blass, Perry Ellis, and Ralph Lauren are preeminent in men's ready-to-wear couture. Suits, jackets, and trousers are fluid and shapely, with an understated flair in cut and detail. A big raglan-sleeved topcoat of camel or alpaca is a city mainstay; heather-colored sweaters, pleated-front trousers, fine-knit polo shirts—they all spell ease. With the addition of a suit or two for formal occasions, lightweight jackets and trousers of silk-and-linen mix, a rugged parka for the great outdoors, the groom is ready for any climate. His wardrobe can be as adaptable as the bride's, and help confirm his image of himself as a newly minted husband.

THE HONEYMOON

Whatever anyone may say about adventurous honeymoon trips, most couples settle for sun, beach, and relaxation after the hectic pace of the previous weeks. Unwinding, rather than cliff climbing or storming European capitals, is a wise choice, but this is up to the individuals concerned. A trip to Africa or French Polynesia are exhilarating options for those with the time and money to spare.

The word "honeymoon" evolved from an ancient tradition among Germanic tribes, where the newlyweds sipped honey-sweetened mead every day from one moon to the next, in month-long celebration. Times have changed: couples today spend an average of eight to nine days away, according to travel agents. Which leaves a career couple with two or three days free upon return to settle in.

People continue to honeymoon where people always have: in the Caribbean, Bermuda, Florida, Hawaii, California, and Mexico. "Now that you've found Mr. Right, don't take him on the wrong honeymoon," exhorts a popular advertisement, to prove that the bride usually makes the final choice. She wants de luxe comfort and great food in a sylvan or shore-front setting, as well as the security of a well-established location. The greater general interest in food has resulted in hotels, ski and beach resorts offering better cuisine than ever.

But, as in every worthwhile undertaking, you must make long-range plans. Your honeymoon trip is slated for lifelong memories, so you want to be certain of the best possible season. The surest way is to book everything through top-class travel agents. Their advice and expertise are invaluable; for honeymooners who have had much on their minds, a virtual necessity. They will take over the worry of the travel arrangements entirely, and if anything goes awry can find a speedy solution.

If you plan a winter wedding and dream of honeymooning in the Caribbean or some other popular spot, book a year-plus in advance. For spring and fall trips allow six months in advance, and for a summer honeymoon plan nine months ahead. If one of you is not a regular sailor, think before booking a cruise. There has been many a seasick bride. If you want a few thrills, have the agent arrange a location that balances leisure hours with para-sailing, wind-surfing, or ballooning. Later or second-time marrieds might prefer a slow-tempo exploration of ancient sites or cities to lying on a beach. Whatever your notion of an ideal escape, an all-inclusive package can be tailored to suit your budget.

As for travel details, you will of course have insured your jewelry and clothes. Take hand luggage on board the airplane and keep valuables, documents, and immediate necessities with you in case your luggage strays for a day or two. If the distances are not too great, telephone your parents after you arrive to thank them again for a beautiful wedding day.

If the management knows you are honeymooners, you will receive gifts of champagne, flowers, and chocolates in your room. Some hotels offer free saunas for two, and the chef's special menu to honeymooning couples. So expect treats.

THANK-YOU NOTES

Officially, a guest has up to one year's grace in which to send a wedding present. The wise bride keeps track of the gifts as they arrive, and writes a thank-you note immediately. Or, if the preceding weeks are too hectic, devise a numbering system with stickers on each present, and record them on a tally list. After the nuptials, your new husband can share the task of writing the thank-you notes, which should be completed within three months of your wedding day. Thank-you notes are always handwritten, on your personal stationery. They are usually signed in one name, making reference to the other: "Peter and I thank you . . ." Stationery monogrammed with the bride's married initials will be versatile for use after the thank-yous are done.

YOUR FIRST DINNER ALONE

The return home to the realities of every day need not deflate the magic. If you were carried over the threshold, you fooled the evil spirits who try to trip the bride at the door—once considered very unlucky. Keep the mood of romance alive by planning a very special homecoming dinner for two. He can cook for you, or you for him. Dress as if it is your first date; lavish the table with flowers, candles, and your best new china and crystal. Open a fabulous bottle of wine, sit back and enjoy the luxury of private time together. Rekindle the spirit of moments like these: make a family tradition of an intimate, candlelit supper alone with your husband from time to time. Well after the babies are asleep.

YOUR FIRST DINNER PARTY

You want your first dinner party in your new setting to be perfect. A good host and hostess meet the challenge by planning ahead and working together. This is the chance to use your new cookbooks, and to set out the wedding gift tableware. Two or three days beforehand, order the wine, cocktail mixes, cordials, and ice for delivery. If you plan a spectacular entrée, keep the other courses simple. Put good, crusty bread on the table, with sweet butter; have plenty of mineral water in stock for non-wine drinkers. Offer fresh fruit for the guest who doesn't eat desserts.

This is an occasion for close family and friends, who want to hear about the honeymoon trip and enjoy your homecoming. If you burn the soup, whip out that standby jar of caviar. Nobody will mind.

Patricia Warner

*T*he choice of the engagement ring is almost as personal a commitment as the choice of a fiancé. As a tangible, enduring, and highly visible proof of love, it must be the one ring the bride and groom both want to symbolize their engagement.

The next choice, stationery to announce the future wedding, invite the guests, and eventually thank friends and relations for presents, is less personal.

The wedding is a celebration that embraces all age groups and two often imperfectly matched sets of relations and friends. Engraved contact with them is best when it follows the formality and established etiquette required by group communication.

Once engaged and with the wedding date set, it is time for the bride-to-be to seek the informed, professional help of bridal registry consultants and select the patterns of china, crystal, silver, linens, and housewares that best correspond to her tastes and her fiancé's and to the lifestyle both have dreamed of and are planning.

The newlyweds, not their friends and relations, will be living with the wedding presents; they should be the appropriate props to bring enjoyment, glamour, and a sense of event to the daily ceremonies of their lives.

Then there are the entertainments and family gatherings following the engagement, and they should all be decorated and catered to reflect the joy, the enthusiasm, and the romanticism of the moment.

CHAPTER I

· · · · · · · ·

The Engagement

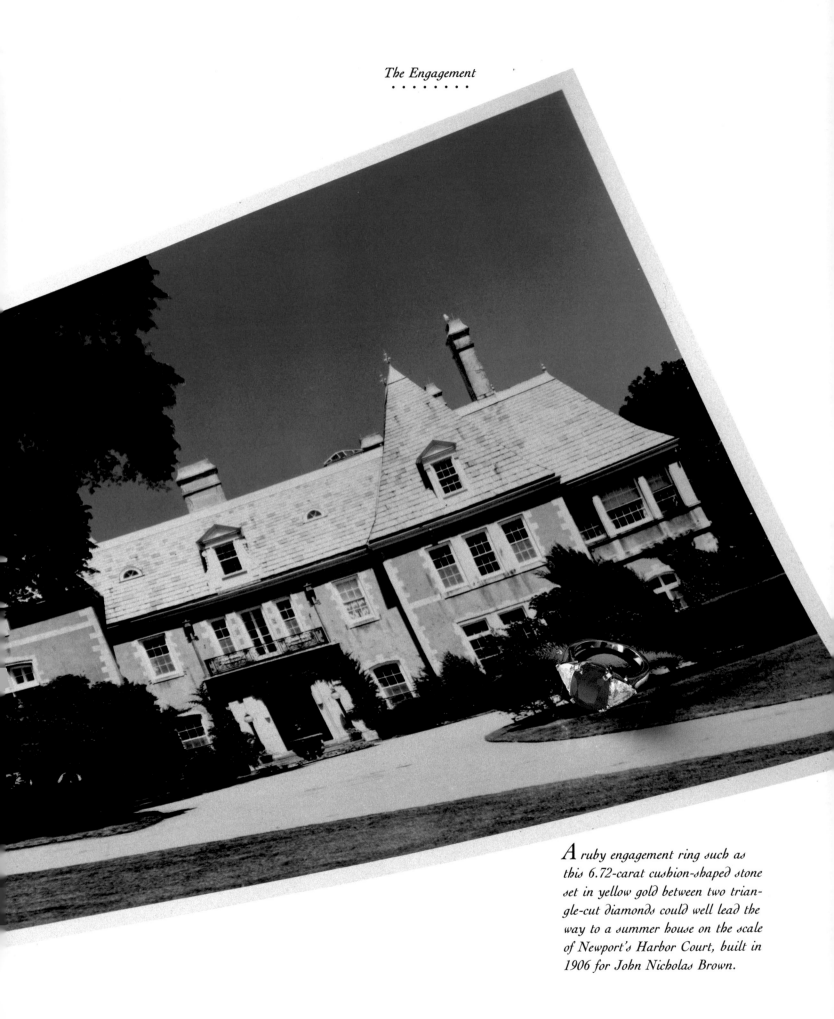

A ruby engagement ring such as this 6.72-carat cushion-shaped stone set in yellow gold between two triangle-cut diamonds could well lead the way to a summer house on the scale of Newport's Harbor Court, built in 1906 for John Nicholas Brown.

The two tapered baguette diamond side stones of this Tiffany ring complement the geometry of this 8.5-carat emerald-cut emerald shown here before the entrance of the Jordan Winery in California's Alexander Valley.

*T*he sapphire runs second after the diamond in popularity as an engagement ring. Shown against the approach to the Auchincloss family's Hammersmith Farm in Newport, this oval sapphire weighs 8.53 carats and is set in platinum with two triangular diamond side stones.

The traditional diamond solitaire engagement ring may or may not have side stones. This Tiffany ring holding a fine Extra, Extra, Extra River pear-shaped diamond guarding the drive to Newport's Marble House weighs 11.37 carats, is of VS1 clarity, and has two pear-shaped side diamonds weighing 2.03 carats.

The Engagement

In the role of stationer, Tiffany offers not only the classic invitation plain or paneled in London script, Belgrave script, or shaded antique Roman, but fill-in invitations, notepapers, and cards, calling and reception cards, monogrammed matchbooks, menus, gift enclosure cards, and place cards.

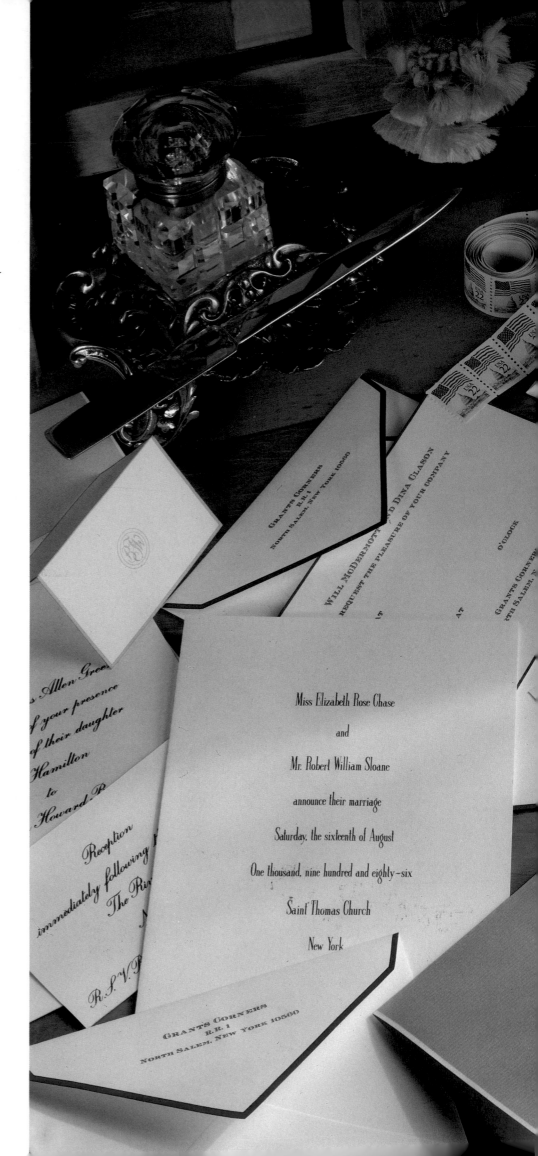

Miss Elizabeth Rose Chase

and

Mr. Robert William Sloane

announce their marriage

Saturday, the sixteenth of August

One thousand, nine hundred and eighty-six

Saint Thomas Church

New York

*T*he Pinkerton Ranch engagement
dinner, for all its innocent home atmosphere, has been expertly catered
by Caroly Pettyjohn of Dallas's
Party Service Inc. Food is hearty and
typically Texan: barbecued ribs and
fried chicken served in an enameled
iron basin, T-bone steaks and boiled
new potatoes, boiled corn and onions
served on Tiffany stoneware platters,
boiled carrots in a "Tiffany Yellow
Flowers" ironstone bowl, sweet-sour
pickled pears, and strawberry cream
in a red cabbage. To drink there is
Texas classic "long-neck" Lone Star
beer.

Wild flowers from the banks of
nearby Ten Mile Creek are held in
Tiffany ceramic pitchers and an old
family ice-cream freezer.

The groom's family's first gift to
the bride-to-be, an Elsa Peretti silver
snake belt, ornaments the table.

Wild grasses and yarrow are rus-
tic rings for antique lace napkins.

Displayed on the dining-room table of the house Frank Lloyd Wright built in 1889, when he was twenty-two, for his new bride Catherine Tobin in Oak Park, Illinois, are china, crystal, and silver designed by Wright, the greatest of all American architects. Produced by Tiffany & Co. under the auspices of The Frank Lloyd Wright Foundation, they set an example of coherence and individuality in table furnishings.

The stylishly colorful porcelain as well as the silver coffee set, tureen and salt and pepper shakers were all part of Wright's designs for Tokyo's 1916 old Imperial Hotel.

The hexagonal crystal candlesticks came later, and the Wright "sky-scraper" terra-cotta vase was designed in the first years of the century. Following Mr. Wright's fondness for weeds, Chicago florist Virginia Wolff has filled it with dill, blue dust flowers, thistles, night-shade, cattail leaves, physostegia, and blue nigella.

facing page

A background of Pratesi signature hand-embroidered eyelet sheets, pillow covers, and a white-on-white chain-patterned bedcover inspires New York's La Lingerie's trousseau of white and peach. Included here are the lace-trimmed silk satin night-gown and peignoir the bride will wear on her wedding night and her Koos Van Den Akker lingerie case.

*T*his restrained and stylish setting of Tiffany's "Hampton" flatware, "Celadon" French porcelain, "Victoria" globlets, and "Dom Pérignon" flute champagne glasses is anchored by a Tiffany silver Doric column candlestick. It could work as well with classic Georgian or Art Deco-inspired contemporary surroundings.

*D*emonstrating the versatility of neo-classicism in its many urbane and coolly self-assured guises, this mannered and formal setting by interior design team Joan Glacken and Gerardo Yavar mixes Tiffany's "San Lorenzo" sterling flatware with the strictly ordered radial gold and black Louis XIV chinoiserie pattern of "Nuit Chinoise" Private Stock porcelain.

The octagonal service plate, Adams style coffee service, and Doric column candlestick are all from Tiffany's collections of sterling silver.

*"T*iffany Swag" English cut crystal, "Hamilton" flat silver, a "cane cut" bucket vase, and the robust and simple wreath of "Napoleon Ivy" plates work in harmony with a Lee Jofa English flowered chintz tablecloth to create a comfortably formal English country table.

facing page

*N*amed for a beautiful French fishing village on the Normandy coast, Tiffany's "Honfleur" ovenproof earthenware is as at home in a relaxed country setting as it is here, used for a dinner of determined formality. Its Louis XV style conforms to the grandeurs of the Tiffany silver pumpkin tureen and palm candlesticks, and harmonizes with the "Provence" crystal goblets and "Flemish" flat silver.

*P*rominent New York and New Jersey interior designer Mrs. John ("Nancy") Pierrepont sets her charm-laden tea table with Tiffany's "Biedermeier" hand-painted Austrian potteries whose universally popular pink and green roses have been in fashion since the mid-nineteenth century.

The Biedermeier style was designed as "Everyman's style" and has long succeeded on that footing.

A Miriam Slater portrait of the Pierreponts' dogs Pounce and Arabella supervises the tea party.

The fresh, direct little blue cornflowers on Tiffany's "Villandry" Limoges porcelain have been a perennially popular motif since the late eighteenth century when they symbolized democracy to the French. Informally strewn across plates with a small-scale formal wreath border, they lend themselves to a broad range of stylistic interpretations.

Tiffany's "Audubon" flat silver and "Tiffany Swag" crystal join "Villandry" porcelain in this setting with its informal chinoiserie décor.

*T*iffany's Private Stock "Framboise Rose" porcelain, "Bamboo" silverware, and "Rock Cut" crystal candlesticks and silver bowl were all designed by Van Day Truex and bear his mark of boldness combined with simplicity and color and designs derived from natural forms and patterns.

facing page

*T*he zanily elegant gestures of Pattern Painting are a thoroughly American and thoroughly delightful manifestation of contemporary art.

In these porcelain tablewares designed by celebrated New York ceramist Dorothy Hafner for Tiffany & Co., the sticks and checks and stripes and dots and dashes of pattern animate a setting of Tiffany "Faneuil" flat silver and flaring "Victoria" stemware.

The combination of black with saturated pastel decorator colors allows Dorothy Hafner's "Confetti" dishes to be dressed up or down according to the occasion.

The equally adaptable Post-Modernist chairs designed by Robert Venturi are from Knoll International.

*T*he spirited black and white stripes and checks of New York potter Beth Forer's inlaid ceramics made for Tiffany & Co. complement the clear surfaces of modern design. They are equally harmonious with the American colonial simplicity of Tiffany's "Salem" flat silver, capstan salt and peppers, and paneled coffee service.

facing page

*F*or a bridal shower luncheon party, the present Mrs. Benjamin Harrison decorated this gazebo overlooking the James River at the ancestral home of the Harrisons, Berkeley Plantation. Mrs. Harrison's suspended, beribboned floral "centerpiece" gives a buoyantly festive air to the party.

Royal Crown Derby china, used to complement the bowed and skirted table, and the gilt ballroom chairs are from Taylor Hogan Fine Interiors in nearby Richmond.

The flat silver is Tiffany's "Shell and Thread."

page 118

"*T*he best wedding gifts are those that excite us personally," says Charles Paxton Gremillion of Dallas's treasure emporium Loyd-Paxton. Here gifts at a bridal shower include a French Directoire mahogany urn-shaped clock dated 1795, a carved colored stone toucan, and an English Regency tortoiseshell box inlaid with silver, all from Loyd-Paxton, as well as a classic French carriage clock, Private Stock porcelains, and a crystal decanter reproduced from an original in the collection of the Marquess of Bath at Longleat, all from Tiffany & Co.

page 119

*O*n the terrace of the Dallas, Texas, urban villa that houses the fabled Loyd-Paxton gallery, a marble table base designed by Thomas Hope supports a round section of ancient Roman flooring on which is displayed the buffet for an evening bridal shower.

Andrea Whitefield's Dallas "Food Company" has provided the massed calla lilies, skewers of tuna and swordfish marinated and grilled with orange peppers, and the oriental vegetables with sesame vinaigrette in radicchio leaves tied with a scallion. The simple but colorful food is served on gadrooned silver platters from Tiffany's "Treasures from Stately Homes" collection. The champagne glasses are tied with white satin bows.

The gilt chairs were designed by Robert Adam for Harewood House.

facing page

The Morvan stud is world-famed for breeding and raising racehorses such as triple-crown winner and Hall of Fame thoroughbred "Shuvee." The Morvan gardens breed and raise oversized single peonies, oriental poppies, and bearded iris of almost artificial perfection.

A painted garden basket is filled with these Morvan beauties to decorate the setting of a bridesmaids' luncheon which will also feature brightly wrapped gifts from Richmond, Virginia's, Cachet Ltd.

Cachet's luncheon table in the Morvan formal garden is centered around a dapper, flower-bedecked Cachet pottery rabbit and set with Strasbourg tulip plates and Tiffany & Co. "Shell and Thread" flat silver, a perennial bridal favorite. There is a gift for each bridesmaid of a Tiffany-designed English enamel flowered box as a keepsake of the celebration.

Morvan is situated at the foot of Carter's Mountain. In the early days of the Virginia colony, it belonged to the Carters.

The bridesmaids will lunch on shad roe, wild asparagus, pommes de terre soufflées, Sally Lunn bread, and fresh raspberries with homemade French vanilla ice cream and paper-thin oatmeal cookies.

Thomas Jefferson drew the plans for Mrs. Whitney Stone's home, Morvan, built in 1820 just three and a half miles down President's Road from Monticello, and Jefferson may have had a hand in the design of the distinguished formal garden.

Here the garden is the scene of a bridesmaids' luncheon designed by Ann Page and Mary Anne Hooker of Cachet Ltd. in Richmond. The unbridled romanticism of the Cachet style is evident in the flowered and striped skirting and bows and embroidered openwork top cloth that set the bridal mood.

facing page

Mrs. William McCormick Blair's table is set with Tiffany "Shell and Thread" flat silver, open basket-weave Este earthenware plates, and "All Purpose" wineglasses for a pre-nuptial agreement lunch. The table-cloth is hand-painted Chinese silk. Porcelain vegetables by Lady Anne Gordon sit at the foot of a bouquet of white peonies and lilacs similar to those the bride will carry at the wed-ding. Mrs. Blair wisely observes that such extreme refinement for an essentially legal discussion is "improbable but instructive."

Mrs. William McCormick Blair sets a mood of determined elegance in her Washington, D.C., home's din-ing room for a prenuptial agreement lunch, where the bride and her lawyer and the groom and his lawyer discuss mutually reassuring property divi-sions before the wedding. The extreme grace of the setting encourages the diplomacy demanded on such occa-sions.

*T*he wedding celebrates a passion for life and the best it offers that is enthusiastically shared by all present at the ceremony.

The wedding's script is always familiar and rightfully discourages improvisation; however, the stage, the music, the set, and the costumes offer broad possibilities for personal taste and to family or community tradition.

But wherever taste and tradition may lead, weddings should be designed and dressed to visually nourish a dreamlike quality that will reconcile the important features of the day into a storybook world of harmony and delight.

There is a deliberateness and sophistication in the wedding's function of reconfirming long-established values, but there must also be an instinctive, comfortable, and natural style to the event that lifts it above simple ceremony. That style may be very grand or very simple; both have the ability to charm and delight.

The wedding's location, its decorations, the clothes, and the objects that commemorate it must be selected to celebrate both ceremony and style.

CHAPTER II
· · · · · · · ·
The Wedding

In a delightful garden setting,
House Beautiful *editor JoAnne
Barwick creates a luncheon to plan
the perfect garden wedding. Books on
flowers and gardening will be consulted, sketches made of the ideal floral décor, gardeners and local nurs-
ery experts will be consulted and
actual flowers used to coordinate the
colors, shapes, textures, and proportions of flowers needed to achieve the
desired effect.*

*On the table "Fleur sur Fond
Gris," Tiffany Private Stock china,
is appropriately used with "Provence"
flat silver.*

above

*F*lorist Tom Rogers of Boston's Tommy has decorated the gracefully columned neocolonial chapel of Middlesex School near Concord, Massachusetts, for a spring wedding with pew bows and bouquets of white casablanca lilies, sweet peas, asparagus fern, and ruscus leaves, all tied with satin ribbon bows.

right

*I*n the middle of a secluded lake in California's Napa Valley, on the enchanted island retreat of Anita Mardikian and her Austrian painter husband Pepo Pickler, a polychromed terra-cotta Chinese shrine serves as the site for a California garden wedding.

A Tiffany vermeiled sterling silver Regency birdcage ornaments the lawn, as do pink and white water lilies picked at the foot of the island's stone-covered embankment.

Alva Erskine Smith was born the daughter of a Mobile, Alabama, cotton planter. She married William K. Vanderbilt who built her America's most lavish summer home, Marble House in Newport, whereupon she divorced him three years later and married Oliver Hazard Perry Belmont.

Here in Alva Vanderbilt's bedroom at Marble House, Mary McFadden shows designs for the bride: for the rehearsal dinner-dance her "Raj" dress, a short-sleeved white sheath with a deep square neckline completely embroidered with sequins and beads with copper accent trim; for the wedding her "Elizabeth Rex" ivory "Marii" pleated evening robe with golden embroidered bodice which combines long sleeves and a squared neckline with an Elizabethan dropped waist and columnar skirt.

*W*hen William Watts Sherman's daughter Mildred married Ralph Julian Stonor, Fifth Lord Camoys, on November 25, 1911, she became the eighteenth American to marry a British peer, following in the footsteps of Consuela Vanderbilt, Mary Goelet, Helen Gould . . .

When their daughter Mildred Noreen Stonor married John R. Drexel III on January 11, 1941, she wore this long-trained silver lamé wedding dress designed by Herman Patrick Patté and pictured in the Van Alen Memorial Room of Newport's palatial summer "cottage" The Elms, built for Philadelphia coal magnate Edward J. Berwind in 1901.

Interspersed with a collection of Tiffany porcelain boxes, family photos on the writing table show Mrs. Drexel in her wedding dress and driving to her wedding wearing a traditional wedding crown of flowers and wheat, as well as family gatherings at Stonor, the ancestral home of Mrs. Drexel's family for eight hundred years.

*T*his old-fashioned China silk bridal gown from America's ever-popular designer of bridal fashions, Priscilla of Boston, features leg-o'-mutton sleeves, basque waist, and a ballgown skirt.

The American colonial style of Priscilla of Boston's gown is echoed by the painted wainscoting and woodblocked Chinese tree-patterned wallpaper of the Belfry Bedroom of the Sleeper McCann House in Gloucester, Massachusetts.

The bridal bouquet by Tom Rogers of Boston's Tommy florists is of casablanca lilies, ruscus, and coffee foliage. To hold the ample wedding veil, Priscilla of Boston provides a headpiece ornamented with China silk roses.

*A*ssured elegance and unbounded romance join forces in these ruffled organza bride's and bridesmaid's dresses by Oscar de la Renta shown in John Loring's Manhattan Georgian apartment.

The bride's gown is white silk organza with multiple rows of bias ruffles with puffed sleeves and a cathedral train. The bridesmaid's gown is satin lace and dotted antique pink organza, ballerina length, with a v-ruffled bodice, dropped waistline, and ballroom sleeves.

Mr. Loring's William Kent settee, upholstered in blue and white pillow ticking, holds the bride's silk flower and organza ruffle crown, her long and voluminous tulle veil, and her bridesmaid's pink organza hat.

Bouquets of white lilac and lisianthus in blue-and-white late Ming vases sit on the mantel. Casablanca lilies, delphiniums, lisianthus, and aronia roses fill the fireplace, all deftly arranged by Renny of New York.

A James Herring painting of horses and barnyard animals hangs above the fireplace.

*F*or the spring bride, Carolina Herrera designs a white silk dress with puffed and vertically ruffled taffeta skirt and tailored gathered silk bodice, shown here in the Washington bedroom of Mrs. William McCormick Blair. Carolina Herrera's bride will wear a short veil of white tulle attached to a gathered silk headpiece, white satin pumps with satin ribbon rosette bows, and will carry an informal bouquet of white peonies and white lilacs.

facing page

*F*or a small but formal evening wedding, the groom's black double-
breasted dinner clothes are laid out
on Napoleon's mahogany and ormolu
campaign bed in the guest room of
Dallas's quintessential dealers in
works of art, Charles Paxton Gremillion and Loyd Ray Taylor. Tab-
lets concealed in a secret round
drawer of Napoleon's bed are unfolded
to hold the groom's pearl and gold
Schlumberger "acorn" stud and
cufflink set and "Classic" watch,
both from Tiffany & Co.

*C*hampagne in a remarkable cooler
in the Russian style made by the
great French bronze maker and
enameler Ferdinand Barbedienne in
the mid-1800s, a "Laurelton Hall"
crystal champagne flute, a Viennese
paste-and-enamel frame holding a
portrait of the bride, and an antique
English frame holding a portrait of
the groom's pet Weimaraner are
thoughtfully provided by Loyd-Paxton for the groom as he dresses in

their Dallas guest room. There are
100 white carnations from which to
choose a boutonnière. And as an addition to the newlyweds' first home,
there is an equestrian bronze of
Louis XIV by Girardon, identical to
the one Louis XIV himself had
placed in the rotunda of Vaux-le-
Vicomte for him to consider.

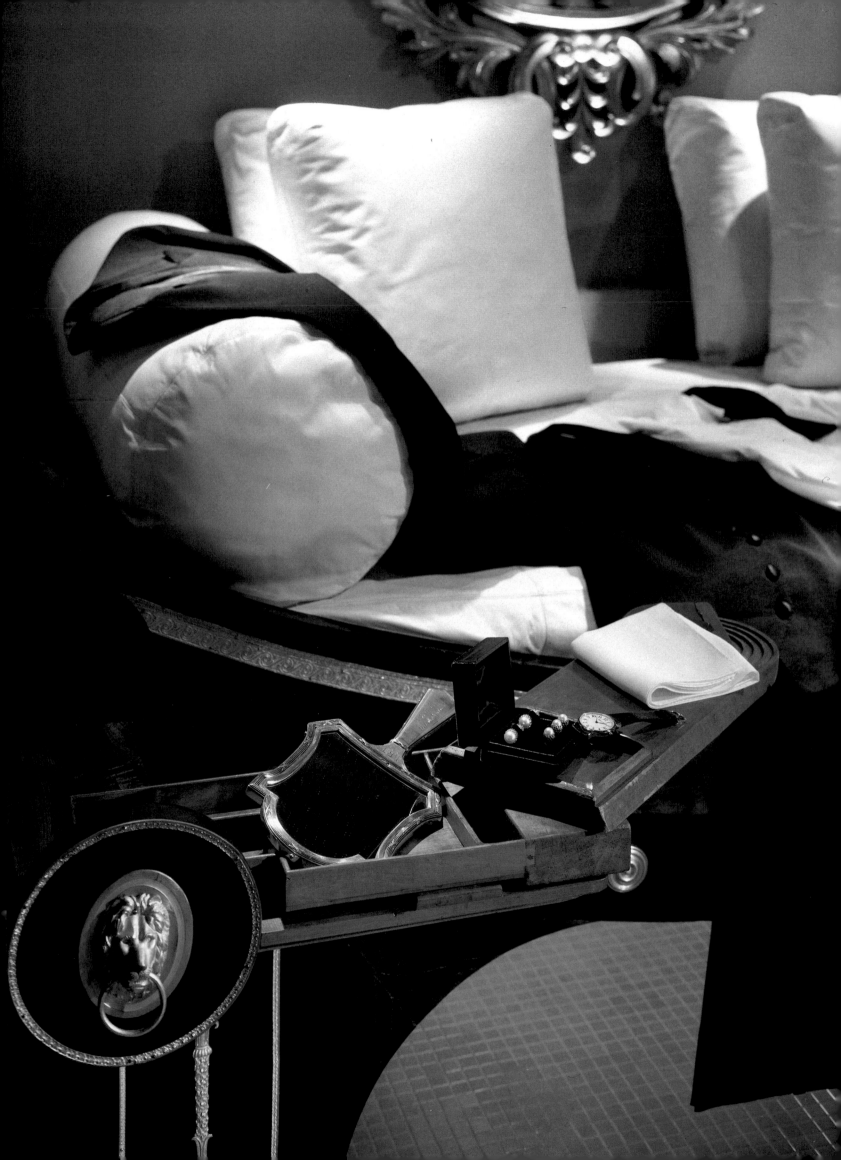

facing page

*F*or the civil wedding, John Weitz proposes this blue chalk-striped suit, a white-collared blue and white broad-striped shirt, and a solid blue tie accessorized by a white Irish linen handkerchief and pink carnation.

The Weitz groom stands outside Manhattan's Municipal and Civil Court Building. His "bride" is dressed in the front-pleated, long-sleeved, dove-gray dress with a gray-and-white-striped bow-tie neck and a white straw hat with a giant silk rose, both from Saks Fifth Avenue. America's "last" Astor, Jacqueline, wore these for her Manhattan Municipal and Civil Court Building wedding to Nicholas Drexel.

A bridal bouquet of white and yellow freesias sits on the picket fence.

*O*ver five hundred guests attended Consuelo Vanderbilt's coming-out party at Marble House on August 28, 1895. Her future husband, the Duke of Marlborough, was conveniently a houseguest at the time and proposed to the debutante that evening.

Here in the Vanderbilts' guest room occupied by the Duke, Bill Blass shows a groom's classic morning suit.

Tiffany silver accessories sit on the dresser where the ninth Duke of Marlborough once groomed himself for that momentous evening at Marble House.

*Amidst the gleaming mahogany
of the legendary sailing yacht
Santana's aft cabin, a Ralph
Lauren double-breasted blue wool
blazer with brass anchor buttons,
white flannel trousers, white shirt,
red-and-blue-striped tie, white handkerchief, and white laced bucks are
laid out for the groom to dress for a
shipboard wedding.*

*The dresser holds Tiffany silver
men's accessories: a shoehorn, a
hairbrush, a comb, a perpetual calendar, a photo frame, and a stainless
steel Tiffany "Diver's Watch."*

*The photos are of the Santana's
former owner, Humphrey Bogart,
and his wife Lauren Bacall.*

The Wedding
· · · · · · · ·

left

In November 1895, Mrs. William K. Vanderbilt realized a Gilded Age society mother's dream when her eighteen-year-old daughter Consuelo married the ninth Duke of Marlborough.

Here in Consuelo Vanderbilt's bedroom in Newport's Marble House, Geoffrey Beene shows designs for a contemporary mother of the bride.

Mr. Beene's daytime three-piece ensemble has a gray organza short skirt and bolero jacket with short sleeves and satin piping. Both are trimmed with wide scalloped lace and are to be worn with a pale gray silk taffeta blouse with scalloped hem and sleeves edged in gray lace.

For evening, Mr. Beene shows an emerald-green striated silk ankle-length dress with long sleeves, fitted bodice, and a full skirt with trapunto stitching at the hem and cuffs, to be worn with a wide stitched wrap belt with pompons.

overleaf

At Newport's Rosecliff, the Grand Trianon-inspired white-glazed terra-cotta mansion built in 1902 by Stanford White for Mrs. Hermann Oelrichs, the lacy splendors of wedding clothes by the celebrated bridal fashion designer Pat Kerr stand for their portrait on the front lawn. The bride's "ecru tulle fantasy gown" has a sweeping train of blush pink Carrickmacross lace that attaches at the shoulders. The bridesmaid's ecru silk taffeta gown has jaunty shoulder ruffles. There is an ecru lace "little girl's dress" for the flower girl. Both she and the bridesmaid will wear Pat Kerr's beribboned orange blossom headpieces. The ring bearer will wear an ecru shirt with moiré knickers and silk taffeta sash.

This assortment of Tiffany & Co.'s suggested gifts for attendants includes, for the bridesmaids: "Coeur Fleur" and "Halcyon" Private Stock porcelain boxes; Paloma Picasso sterling silver "X" earrings and a "scribble" pin; Tiffany's exclusive Baccarat "Artichoke" bud vase; a Louis Comfort Tiffany-inspired Battersea enamel box; and an Elsa Peretti split ring "Peretti Heart" key ring. For the groomsmen there are: sterling silver and 14k gold engine-turned belt buckles; Schlumberger 18k gold "Love Knot" cuff links; 14k gold barbell cuff links; an engine-turned 14k gold pocket knife; a Tiffany silver beaker, and a sterling silver engine-turned money clip. For both there are Tiffany's famous "Screwball" key rings or "T-clip" pens in sterling silver or 14k gold; an engine-turned sterling silver picture frame; and a Tiffany silver shell ashtray or perpetual calendar.

The pink and yellow rose-and-mimosa bridesmaid's bouquet is by New York's Valorie Hart Designs.

JANUARY

S	M	T	W	T	F	S
		1	2	3	4	5
6	7	8	9	10	11	12
13	14	15	16	17	18	19
20	21	22	23	24	25	26
27	28	29	30	31		

facing page

The handsomely proportioned library of the Richard S. Reynolds III house in Richmond, Virginia, is set for a small bachelor dinner with Crown Staffordshire "Hunting Scene" china and Tiffany "Shell and Thread" flat silver.

The Virginia fox-hunting theme is carried out by a centerpiece of Royal Copenhagen foxes, hunting horse napkin rings, and a painted wood fox waiter holding mint juleps in Tiffany silver beakers.

A Chinese export ware "rose medallion" covered dish and nineteenth-century Coalport plates ornament the room's mantelpiece.

overleaf

Built for William Lyman Stuart of Union Oil in 1935, the 55-foot sailing yacht Santana has been described as a "lady with a past." Today the pride of San Francisco architects Theodore and Thomas Eden, she has belonged to Dick Powell and June Allyson, to Ray Milland, and for twelve years to Humphrey Bogart, whose attachment to her Lauren Bacall described as "enslaved."

Once famed for "Bogie's" stag parties, the Santana is here the locale for a bachelor dinner.

The table is set with "Celadon" plates, "Hamilton" flat silver, and "Tiffany Swag" glasses—the last presumably for the scotch that Bogart claimed gave the Santana her speed when under sail.

Red, white, and blue bachelor buttons center the table in a Tiffany silver "Wave" bowl. The scene is illuminated by Tiffany's crystal "Twinelights."

The racing cup trophy in the background was three times won by the Santana.

left

The fine and nuanced Jordan Chardonnay and Cabernet Sauvignon drunk at this bachelor dinner held in the dining room of the Jordan Winery in California's Alexander Valley were aged in the oak casks seen through the glazed doors beyond the table.

The dining room is handsomely decorated with an army of roses grown at the Jordan Winery.

The wine-loving groomsmen have presented the groom with a sterling silver "Bacchus" flask from Tiffany's.

above

The handsome Wedgwood "Napoleon Ivy" dishes in this setting were designed for Napoleon's use on St. Helena after his defeat at Waterloo. They are combined with Tiffany's "Hampton" flat silver and oversized English cut-crystal goblets from Tiffany's "Treasures from Stately Homes Collection."

The armchair is a reproduction from Baker Furniture's "Stately Homes Collection" of an original in Stratfield Saye House that belonged to the victor of Waterloo, the first Duke of Wellington.

facing page

For a spring bridesmaids' luncheon, Gourmet Magazine's editor Jane Montant sets her table with Tiffany's "Wyndham" flat silver, Venetian "Luciano" goblets, and "Grape Vine" hand-painted Italian ceramic plates. A Tiffany silver basket planted with miniature roses centers the charmingly patterned table.

Inspired by Thomas Jefferson's gardens at the University of Virginia, the Atlanta garden of Thomas E. Martin, Jr., makes an ideal setting for a bridesmaids' luncheon where each bridesmaid will receive a Tiffany silver picture frame from the bride-to-be. The frames are used here as place-card holders around a fanciful floral and topiary centerpiece by Atlanta's Marvin Gardens Designs Ltd., who have also provided the

flower-crowned cherubs.

Raspberry soup with white chocolate shavings from Atlanta's Affairs To Remember is served in Tiffany "Blue Dragon" porcelain.

Tiffany's exclusive "Nemours" Baccarat crystal sparkles in the Georgia sunshine.

The Wedding
· · · · · · · ·

The side porch of Mrs. China Robbins Loring's picturesque all-American "Red House" in Lawrence, Michigan, is set here for a formal country bridesmaids' luncheon.

The Red House's best yellow-and-pink Ludwigsburg porcelain dishes and antique gold-monogrammed Baccarat wineglasses have been brought out for the occasion. The flat silver is Tiffany "Olympian," first introduced in 1880 when the Red House was only thirty years old.

The bridesmaids have each received a Battersea enamel "Red House" box from Tiffany's depicting the site of their luncheon.

Their gift to the bride-to-be is a silver, gold, and sapphire heart pin from Tiffany's "Back To Glamour" collection.

A selection of Tiffany & Co. bride-to-groom and groom-to-bride gifts includes, for the groom, an "Atlas" watch and men's round "Tiffany Classic" watch with arabic number dial and a Schlumberger "Acorn" stud and cuff-link set in 18k gold and hematite. For the bride there is a Schlumberger 18k gold and diamond "Leaves" ring; an opera-length string of 8mm cultured pearls; Paloma Picasso "X" platinum 18k gold and diamond earrings with black pearl drops; platinum and diamond "Swirl" earrings, a pear-shaped diamond pendant, and a platinum and diamond line necklace.

The bride's romantic bouquet and the groom's boutonnière are by New York's Very Special Flowers. The bride's satin rose and simulated pearl headpiece is by New York's Debra Jackson.

*T*his is the time for all things brilliant and desirable, for all things fine and pleasurable, the time for party foods and party flowers with their enticing succulence and frivolity, the time for luxury and excess to have their moment.

The parties around a wedding—the bachelor dinner, the rehearsal dinner, the wedding breakfast, the reception itself, and the family dinner after the reception—can be large or small, presented with dazzling ceremony or with informality; but all must give a sense of event and festivity.

The colors, flowers, and foods appropriate to the time, location, and climate should be exploited. Wedding parties are, after all, no places to hold back.

And then there is the wedding cake. Dressed in its frosted finery, made from sugar mixed with fantasy and artistry, its fleeting moment of glory must too be memorable.

CHAPTER III
· · · · · · · ·
The Parties

*I*n the neo-Georgian red dining room of the Richard S. Reynolds III Virginia home, the table for a formal wedding rehearsal dinner has been decorated by popular Richmond florist Ann Wood Carneal with pink rosebuds caught in billowing swags of white tulle.

The pink and white bridal table brings out the romantic side of the American Classic room designed in the late 1920s by architect William Lawrence Bottomley, best known as the architect of New York's River House.

A small separate table is set for the flower girls at this rehearsal dinner in a corner of the Richard S. Reynolds III dining room.

The children will be royally seated on gilded nineteenth-century Austrian palace ballroom chairs, and will be served on elaborately painted late-nineteenth-century Limoges porcelain plates.

Candles in Tiffany "Chrysanthemum" sterling silver holders will light the storybook setting, which features antique silver bouquet holders to be carried at the wedding.

*M*r. and Mrs. Richard S. Reynolds III's classic table for a rehearsal dinner is set with antique Minton china whose pink bows echo the pink and white theme of the evening.

Guests will be served double consommé, miniature crab cakes, rare butterflied lamb chops with miniature garden vegetables, arugula salad with mint, and individual chocolate soufflés.

Miniature pink and white bride's cakes decorate each place.

facing page

"*Old Strasbourg*" *pottery dishes, Tiffany's "Audubon" flat silver, a Biedermeier apple jam jar, and an assortment of Tiffany's Este Italian ceramic baskets and bowls create a relaxed French Provincial atmosphere on this breakfast table designed by Countess Marina de Brantes.*

For a wedding breakfast on Waikiki beach, Executive Chef Gordon Hopkins of The Colony Surf Hotel offers a meal of grilled Opakapaka (Hawaiian pink snapper) fillets served with shrimps, tropical fruits, and fried bananas, scrambled eggs with smoked salmon, and an open tarte of mixed raspberries and papaya.

The buffet plates are Tiffany's "Flying Colors," foods are served in

leaf-lined Tiffany silver baskets, and tropical floral decorations include massed anthuriums, once known in Hawaii as "little boy flowers."

above

*O*n Mrs. Lawrence Copley Thaw's staircase a bronze Louis XVI cherub gets his feet tangled in the extravagantly glamorous floral garlands designed by John Funt, using laurel leaves, tea roses, freesias, floribunda roses, scabiosa, sweet peas, lythrum, and lisianthus.

facing page

*N*ew York fête designer John Funt composed this romantic white, pink, and ivory bride's bouquet with tea roses, floribunda roses, pink bouvardia, and spiraea tied with white satin ribbons.

Here at the foot of Mrs. Lawrence Copley Thaw's staircase it rests on a gilt wood, gauffré velvet-upholstered Charles X footstool.

*N*ew York's master of party design John Funt decorates the stairs of Mrs. Lawrence Copley Thaw's Park Avenue maisonette for an at-home wedding reception where the bride, in time-honored fashion, will throw her bridal bouquet to her bridesmaids and her garter to the groomsmen from the flower-garlanded staircase.

Mrs. Thaw's first-century B.C. Greek marble Venus with a Boy on a Dolphin *joins in the celebra-* tion of love, as do two fine Louis XVI bronze cherubs holding candles.

left

above

The exceptionally fine Late American Victorian barn was built on Wyllie Farm in Livingston County, Illinois, in 1880. It furnishes an ideal backdrop for a country wedding reception.

    The buffet is decorated with local wild flowers, grains, and decorative weeds and grasses in keeping with the sophisticated country setting.

    Two sterling silver cabbage bowls hold iced champagne.

For an Illinois farm-country wedding this three-tiered cake made by the pastry chef of Chicago's Drake Hotel is topped by sugar wedding bells and boasts a variety of spun sugar roses and ribbons.

    It will be served on "Tiffany Yellow Flowers" Mason's ironstone plates and accompanied by champagne drunk from Tiffany's "Nemours" crystal flutes from Baccarat.

facing page

S*ince it was built in 1712 for Virginia's Randolphs, Tuckahoe Plantation has played host to many famous Americans.*

Here the front court of this early Georgian masterpiece, now the home of Mr. and Mrs. Addison B. Thompson, has been decorated by Cachet Ltd. of Richmond for a classic Virginia wedding reception.

A vintage 1880 landau drawn by thoroughbred Percherons, Molly and Tony, has been provided by Carriage Rides of Richmond.

Richmond, Virginia, designer Sarah Branch has decorated a four-tiered wedding cake in basket-weave white frosting and fresh flowers. Following old Virginia tradition, ribbons lead to silver charms embedded in the cake for the bridesmaids to tell their fortunes. One will pull out a silver heart for love; another a horseshoe for good luck.

O*n the front lawn of Tuckahoe Plantation, under a tent of broad blue and white stripes, Ann Page and Mary Anne Hooker of Richmond's Cachet Ltd. have set tables skirted and tied with bows of Cowtan & Tout's gaily colored taffetas.*

Massive formal bouquets of garden peonies and weigela on white pedestals enhance the sense of occasion at this elaborately decorated country wedding.

facing page

*T*he table set for a reception in The Berkeley Plantation dining room centers on a pierced-work silver epergne brimming over with roses, bachelor buttons, violas, tulips, iris, white astilbe, and a variety of pale lilies, all integrated by variegated ivy and deftly arranged by Taylor Mead Interiors of Richmond.

right

A hexagonal Mason's ironstone vase in the Japanese Revival style of the 1870s and '80s decorates the porch of Wyllie Farm's 1880s farmhouse, while waiting to be used on a wedding reception buffet. Tall, gracefully curving heads of timothy grass and stalks of the white Queen Anne's lace that grows at the edges of the Wyllies's surrounding corn and soybean fields dramatize the tall bouquet of delphiniums, liatris, yellow geum, cornflowers, and pink astilbe.

page 178

*T*his informal centerpiece arrangement for a wedding reception at Tuckahoe Plantation is a triumph of country style.

The single peonies, larkspur, foxglove, monkshood, delphinium-blue clematis, snapdragons, Virginia yellowweed, Virginia clover, nerine lilies, sterling star lilies, and astors are all grown in the Tuckahoe Plantation gardens that flower prolifically just to the north of the historic plantation schoolhouse where Thomas Jefferson went to classes.

page 179

*T*he flower girl's basket of country flowers is casually hung on the back of a gilt ballroom chair beside this outdoor reception table at Tuckahoe Plantation set with Tiffany & Co.'s "Audubon" flat silver and "Escalier de Crystal" Private Stock hand-painted French porcelain. Mint tea punch is served in an antique silver goblet to accompany the buffet catered by Barrington of Richmond, consisting of Smithfield ham, beaten biscuits, Chesapeake oysters, creamed Chesapeake crabmeat in puff pastry shells, and home-grown Tuckahoe strawberries.

Jordan almonds symbolize good luck and prosperity.

left

above

Since its opening amidst the "roar" of 1920 Chicago, the imperial splendors of the Drake Hotel's Gold Coast Room have witnessed the dinner dances and receptions of generations of important Chicago weddings.

Here, for an elaborate wedding rehearsal formal dinner dance, a table is set with "Laurelton Hall" and "Gold Ivy" porcelain, "Audubon" vermeil flatware, and "Newport" crystal, all from Tiffany & Co.

For a very formal wedding rehearsal dinner, the Drake Hotel's executive sous-chef, Franz Kranzfelder, prepared lamb noisettes with poached fennel filled with ratatouille, baby carrots, white turnips, confit of shallots cooked in red wine and vinegar, with a fresh tarragon sprig.

A suitably grand gold, diamond, and citrine minaudière designed by Paloma Picasso for Tiffany's joins the setting.

*T*his quietly grand centerpiece designed by Virginia Wolff of Chicago's Floral Creations ingeniously
mixes Tiffany & Co. vermeil flowers
with godetia, floribunda roses, miniature pink calla lilies, cornflowers,
and miniature carnations. All are
contained in a Tiffany vermeil "Ri-
yadh" bowl carrying out the theme of
the Drake Hotel's Gold Coast Room
for which the centerpiece was created.

overleaf

*T*win tables skirted in antique cur-
tain laces hold the bride's cake and
groom's cake for an "at home" reception in the Elton Hyders' Fort Worth
dining room. The fireplace overman-
tel is decked with garlands of leaves
interwoven with silk ribbons, while
the collection of Russian icons looks
down approvingly on the day's
celebration.

THE TIFFANY WEDDING

left

*T*he Southern love of gala occasion and formal dignity is brought into play in Mrs. Dean Day Smith's yellow and white neo-Georgian Atlanta dining room set for a classic wedding reception.

Carrying out the bridal theme, Mrs. Smith has placed porcelain "Orange Blossom Sprays" by Dorothy Doughty beside her yellow, white, and pink floral centerpiece, along with a Meissen porcelain church made in 1748 for Count Heinrich von Bruehl.

The tiered wedding cake from Atlanta's Affairs To Remember will be served on "Flora Danica" plates from Tiffany & Co.

On Mrs. Smith's superb 1810 Boston Sheraton sideboard, Royal Berlin refraîchissoirs hold strawberries next to a pair of gilt swan girandoles that once belonged to Napoleon's brother, Jerome Bonaparte.

overleaf

*I*n the dining room of the house they built on the town square of Lawrence, Michigan, in 1850 the portrait of Ralsman and Betsy Mathilda Hathaway Webster oversees an archetypal American country town wedding reception prepared by their great-granddaughter Mrs. China Robbins Loring.

The wedding cake encrusted with frosting roses from Desserts Unlimited in nearby Paw Paw, Michigan, will be served on the house's original "Mason's No. 1" pattern ironstone dishes and eaten with Tiffany "Chrysanthemum" forks. Green nineteenth-century Bohemian cut-glass coupes are provided for champagne. Matching Bohemian glass compotes hold bouquets of garden roses.

The lace tablecloth is antique Venetian, the pressed crystal dolphin candlesticks are from Tiffany's.

facing page

*A*nita Mardikian's father built an island platform in the Mardikian Ranch's lake in the Napa Valley to support a small Armenian church. His daughter built a bright red Chinese temple of her own design which serves here as the site of a wedding reception, where the oriental theme is expressed by the three-tiered wedding cake decorated by San Francisco caterer Fred Wertheim with gold ribbons and orchids and topped by small skyrockets and other colorful symbols of good luck.

above

*S*an Francisco florist Michael Daigian dramatically punctuates the already color-filled atmosphere of Anita Mardikian's Napa Valley garden pavilion with a towering arrangement of foxtail eremurus lilies, stalky ginger, spiky rex palm fronds, giant green and pink anthuriums, white lilies and brightly exotic hanging heliconia, all standing in a Tiffany French faience trumpet vase.

A Tiffany faience tray holds "Nancy" crystal champagne flutes and a silver stag's head stirrup cup.

*B*acked by the vibrantly colorful garden of the Napa Valley's Mardikian Ranch, a black lacquer tray holds finger foods for a midday wedding reception prepared by San Francisco caterer Fred Wertheim.

Snow pea pods have been piped full of a dill-scented enriched puree of yellow vegetables. Pastry shells hold chef's pâté decorated with tomato puree, black olives, and rosemary sprigs, and miniature hexagonal black and white bread sandwiches are topped with Japanese radish pickle and green olives.

left

T*he opulence and romantic beauty of New York's Sylvia Weinstock's wedding cakes is mythic. Here a quartet of her masterpieces is photographed on the dining-room table of her Soho loft just steps from her kitchens where they were assembled moments before.*

These remarkable cakes' sugar flowers are all edible and are held to the cakes only by the fresh whipped cream frosting.

U*nder the guidance of* House & Garden *editor Denise Otis, Cile Burbidge of Danvers, Massachusetts, "built" this towering pagoda wedding cake which Denise Otis has set against a* trompe l'oeil *sky and treillage with her usual highly civilized flair.*

facing page

For a wedding reception amid the grapevines of the Jordan Vineyard, San Francisco's Fantasia Creations has designed a classic three-tiered wedding cake ornamented with bunches of green and purple grapes.

The cake will be served on Tiffany's Este "Grape" pattern hand-painted earthenware plates and will be accompanied by Jordan Chardonnay.

Roses and grape leaves all grown at Alexander Valley's Jordan Vineyard fill an antique French grape-picking basket as part of the outdoor decorations for a vineyard wedding at Mr. and Mrs. Thomas Nicholas Jordan's famed California winery.

above

*A*s the centerpiece for Mrs. T. Suffern Tailer's small formal Park Avenue dinner party, New York florist ZeZe created this bouquet which includes white bachelor buttons, nicotiana, Queen Anne's lace, delphiniums, thistles, roses, sweet peas, coreopsis, salvia, salmon jewel lilies, and ixias.

The polychromed openwork Dresden porcelain basket is from Tiffany's.

right

*H*olding its own amidst the unabashed grandeurs of the Gold Ballroom in Newport's Marble House, the intricate architecture of a five-tiered wedding cake by Carr's of Barrington, Rhode Island, boasts cascading pastel ribbons and wreaths of miniature flowers between each layer.

This most sumptuous of American reception rooms was completed in 1892 for William K. Vanderbilt by Richard Morris Hunt.

facing page

Gold-and-black Tiffany "Malmaison" porcelain, named after the Empress Josephine's villa on the outskirts of Paris, makes a glamorous background for this salad of mixed field greens with baby corn and corn silk in vinaigrette garnished with figs, blackberries, and warm Parmesan pastry "leaves." Fresh viola and pansy blossoms complete these painterly still lifes by caterer Susan Holland.

The intricate gold, blue, and white mosaic pattern of Tiffany "Manhattan" porcelain surrounds this rich-textured and opulent entrée of roast quail in a nest of brown butter-flavored fettuccine garnished with plump Michigan cherries, roasted orange peppers, quail eggs, and fresh basil leaves.

Plenitude, not sparseness, is the theme of this reception dinner offering by New York caterer Susan Holland.

page 200

Among the gala desserts created by Executive Chef Jean-Francis Mots of Boston's Ritz-Carlton Hotel for reception dinners, his white-chocolate nautilus shell has special panache. Chef Mots's shells appear to float in a coulis of fresh raspberries and are filled with lemon mousse, papaya spears, and kiwi wedges. Tiffany's "Bande Verte" Limoges porcelain is used to present the gala dessert.

page 201

In preparation for a formal reception dinner, the highly decorative and imaginative fare of New York caterer Susan Holland is displayed in her efficiently equipped kitchen. Color is a key in these delicacies, which include quail nested on fettuccine; lobster medallions on sautéed leeks with saffroned beurre blanc ornamented with purple basil, chervil, and nasturtium flowers; and a salad punctuated with pansies.

facing page

Leading New York caterer Glorious Food's chef Jean-Claude Nédélec proposes a reception dinner menu of fresh morel mushrooms sautéed with shallots, served with spaetzle and morel sauce followed by free-range chicken sautéed with rosemary and accompanied by glazed vegetables and three purees: watercress and spinach; carrot; and white turnip and pear.

The dishes are presented in Glorious Food's kitchens on "Flora Danica" porcelain from Tiffany's.

facing page   *left*   *right*

*F*or a summer reception luncheon, Glorious Food's chef Jean-Claude Nédéléc offers a first course of chilled artichoke bottoms filled with beluga caviar and topped with poached quail eggs and sabayon sauce. The main course will be cold loin of veal filled with apricots and pistachio nuts served with a salad of baby vegetables and a second salad of wild rice, cranberries, grapes, walnuts, and orange zest.

*T*he sophisticated fare of R. C. Wilford Catering enlivens many of New York's leading social events. Here, for an evening reception supper, they offer grilled Norwegian salmon steaks served with red onion confit, brussels sprouts sautéed with pancetta, parsleyed Long Island new potatoes, and steamed baby vegetables.

    The meal is dramatized by Tiffany Private Stock "Black Shoulder" porcelain.

    The miniature topiary trees by the fire stand in Royal Berlin "Tiffany Flowers" porcelain buckets.

*D*esserts for a post-reception supper proposed by R. C. Wilford Catering include Bavarian cream served with fresh seasonal berries, pears poached with spices or with red wine and served with hot chocolate sauce and ginger-scented crème anglaise.

    Wilford presents the deserts on Tiffany's jaunty "Flying Colors" hand-painted earthenware plates.

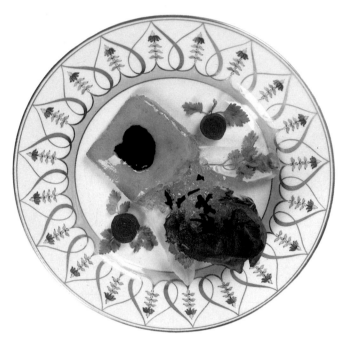

left

*W*edding reception hors d'oeuvre selections, prepared by R. C. Wilford Catering, include seviche of bay scallops and shrimp with mango and papaya served in green and red lettuce leaves, bouchettes of smoked salmon and crème fraîche with chives, tartelettes of Montrachet and sun-dried tomato with fresh basil, and beef carpaccio croustades with garlic herb sauce. All are served on crystal platters from Tiffany & Co.

right

*F*or the first course of a wedding reception luncheon, Jean-Francis Mots, executive chef of Boston's Ritz-Carlton Hotel, composes a colorful and handsome still life on a Tiffany Private Stock "Coeur Fleur" porcelain dinner plate using a generous slice of fresh foie gras en gelée, black truffles, radicchio, endive, Italian parsley, and tomato rosettes.

facing page

*I*n her Danvers, Massachusetts, studio near Boston, Cile Bellefleur Burbidge brings the art of wedding cake decoration to a level of elegance and sophistication that recalls the dazzling Dresden porcelain floral centerpieces made for eighteenth-century European royalty.

The bow-tied garlands and crowning bouquet of this three-tiered cake evoke joy and festivity.

facing page

For a Manhattan garden reception, Colette Peters, a New York designer known for the sophisticated whimsy of her festive party cakes, stacks six cake and frosting "gift boxes" topped by a simulated "blue box" from Tiffany & Co. tied with white sugar ribbons.

Designer Colette Peters details her imaginative wedding cake of stacked frosted-cake "gift boxes" with colorful sugar ribbons and simulates floral printed wrapping paper with piped icing violets.

overleaf

On the lanai of a turn-of-the-century Hawaiian cottage located on the magically beautiful grounds of the Kohala coast's Mauna Lani Bay Hotel, a round table covered in a classic red-and-white Hawaiian print is set for a small wedding reception dinner.

The setting includes "Black Bamboo" plates, "Bamboo" flat silver, "Laurelton Hall" champagne flutes, "Magnolia" pitchers, and "Palm" silver candlesticks, all from Tiffany & Co., as well as halved coconuts filled with poi from Mauna Lani's chef Peter Merriman.

There is a gardenia centerpiece, as well as table ornaments of ti-leaf bows holding frangipani blossoms, and a floral chandelier, all by Hawaii florist Barbara Meheula.

left

Mrs. Elton Hyder uses the grandly proportioned stoa of her Fort Worth home with its vista of the Trinity River Valley as the setting for an after-the-reception family dinner. There will be harp and cello music; and, as night falls, spotlights will illuminate the live oak, hackberry, and pecan trees that grow just beyond the towering columns of the Hyders' dramatic outdoor living area.

overleaf

For her after-the-reception dinner, Mrs. Elton Hyder sets four tables of six with antique silver goblets, Tiffany's "Nemours" champagne flutes, "Chrysanthemum" flat silver, and a mixture of antique china including eighteenth-century Crown Derby Imariware plates; and, on the table in the foreground, Catherine the Great's Sèvres soup plates made for the great tsarina in 1779. A polychromed eighteenth-century Spanish American cupid ornaments each table.

facing page

Pictured in the "Butternut Room" of Newport's Château-sur-Mer, the groom's wardrobe of going-away summer clothes by Perry Ellis includes assortments of spread-collar and button-down-collar shirts and handmade silk ties. There is a navy cotton single-breasted blazer with red and white stripes and a white linen single-breasted blazer; cream-and-emerald cotton pleated trousers, a long-sleeved hand-knit blue cotton cardigan, a tobacco leather belt, white bucks, and brown leather oxfords.

The antique alligator luggage is from New York's Kentshire Galleries, Ltd.

The clock and candlesticks on the mantel as well as the fish-handled "John Drexel" sailing trophy on the side table were all made by Tiffany & Co. in the late nineteenth century.

overleaf

In the bedroom of Mrs. George Peabody Wetmore in Newport's Château-sur-Mer, a Bill Blass trousseau is being packed into Etro "Paisley" luggage. The bride's going-away clothes include a black-and-white beaded Peter Pan-collar shirtdress; a red snakeskin jacket with gold bullion cord trim and crest; a yellow-and-white awning-stripe silk shirtdress; an orange-and-purple wrapped taffeta strapless pouf dress with ankle-strap shirred shoes to match by Manolo Blahnik; an orange linen jacket lined in purple silk crepe; a man-tailored black, white, and red Glen plaid jacket and pants; a bubble-gum pink tucked silk crepe dress; a black-and-white houndstooth crepe coat; a taupe taffeta ball gown with pink, blue, and green woven ribbon bodice, a black cashmere sweater, and navy-and-white spectator pumps by Tanino Crisci.

While packing, the bride will refresh herself with tea from the magnificent silver chinoiserie tea set made by Tiffany, Young & Ellis in 1850.

Cosmopolitan's editor Helen Gurley Brown has outfitted this opulent honeymoon suite for the Cosmo girl with Tiffany silver cabbage bowls holding fruit and an opened Tiffany bracelet box, a Tiffany silver bucket for champagne, "Palm Tree" and "Crab" candlesticks, and "Framboise Rose" Private Stock china. The bride's "La Scala" silk scarf and beaded satin-and-velvet evening bag are also from Tiffany's. Her red satin and black lace nightgown is from Montenapoleone, Inc.

facing page

left

right

*O*nly the legendary creator of the Cosmo *girl*, Helen Gurley Brown, with her sense of luxurious sensuality, could conjure up this honeymoon setting of sybaritic indulgence.

The silver, red, blue, and gold colors, the silky textures, the fleshy lilies, and the red fox coat would surely have delighted the voluptuous dancer in the de Beaulieu painting hanging over the Louis XV daybed.

Tiffany silver-and-vermeil candlesticks light the room which includes a faux leopard-skin bellpull to ring for the servants.

*N*either rice nor rose petals will be thrown after the bride and groom who escape their wedding reception in a Hawaiian outrigger canoe and row across the Mauna Lani lagoons to their island sleeping house.

Well-wishers have filled the bow of the canoe with aromatic island flowers and a silver "Chrysanthemum" champagne cooler and "Laurelton Hall" champagne flutes from Tiffany & Co.

*A*t one side of their sleeping house amid the tropical lagoons of Hawaii's Mauna Lani Bay Hotel, the bride and groom will pause to rest in two koa-wood rocking chairs and have a glass of champagne with a pair of visiting local lovebirds.

The groom's white shirt and red sash are traditional Hawaiian.

The stoneware pitcher holding gardenias, the vermeil candelabra, and "Laurelton Hall" champagne flutes are Tiffany's.

The Honeymoon and After
· · · · · · · ·

*O*n the lagoon-fringed Kohala Coast
of Hawaii in the gardens of the
Mauna Lani Bay Hotel, a small
sleeping house is decorated for the
wedding night.

   The bed is covered with an antique
red-and-white Hawaiian kapa quilt
and hung with mosquito netting.

   A rare antique koa-wood flower
stand is at the foot of the bed holding
fragrant white tropical flowers.

   The bridal crown has been tossed
on the quilt; the simple wedding dress
has been hung from the Psyche
mirror.

   The scene is lit by Tiffany
"Hampton" candlesticks and by the
lyrically beautiful Hawaiian sunset.

In this "well-heeled" private world for newlywed domestic bliss, Bride's Magazine *editor Barbara Tober has provided the bride and groom with every imaginable comfort to face the adventure of writing a seemingly endless list of thank-you notes.*

Special appreciation will be expressed for gifts of a Tiffany "Chrysanthemum" tray and "Chrysanthemum" flat silver, Tiffany Private Stock "Bigouden" porcelain, and the trousseau of antique bed linens from Patrizia Anichini.

left

above

*I*n a peaceful corner of Halston's New York house, the fashion designer has composed a setting for a newlyweds' first dinner at home using silver, crystal, pottery, and carved stone objects all designed by his friend and onetime collaborator Elsa Peretti.

The tranquillity of Halston's bamboo garden, rather than the frenetic activities of the fighting fish in the Hiro photographs behind the table, sets the mood.

*A*n oversized Elsa Peretti heart box dominates Halston's table. The Venetian crystal bowls for caviar, the "Padova" spoons, the black jade butter plate and butter knife, the rock crystal and jade-fobbed drinking cups as well as the two "diamonds-by-the-yard" necklaces offered by the groom to the bride at their dinner were all designed by Elsa Peretti for Tiffany & Co.

The silver heart box was made by Elsa Peretti as a gift for Halston.

THE TIFFANY WEDDING

facing page and right

Playing on the problems inherent in combining households, Architectural Digest's editor-in-chief, Paige Rense, designed this witty table for the first dinner alone of newlyweds with very different tastes in design.

To suit his contemporary taste, his side has a cloth made from a Schumacher Frank Lloyd Wright-designed fabric, Elsa Peretti's "Padova" flatware, and 1930-style Royal Berlin all-white porcelain.

To suit her traditional taste, her side has an antique patchwork quilt tablecover, "Audubon" flat silver designed by Tiffany's Edward C. Moore in 1871, and "Stampino" oven-to-table porcelain.

The trompe l'œil window painting backing the setting is by New York artist Erik Filban.

facing page

*A*n air of civility, warmth, and intimacy pervades this setting by Mrs. T. Suffern Tailer for a small first formal dinner party after the honeymoon.

Mrs. Tailer's table, covered with a damask cloth from Frette Fine Linens, is set with "English King" flatware, "Honeycomb" cut crystal, vermeil service plates, and "Valse Bleu" Private Stock china, all from Tiffany's.

There are individual "Chrysanthemum" silver salt cellars.

John Singer Sargent's painting of the Val d'Aosta hangs on the paisley print upholstered wall behind the table.

page 236

A taste for the simple forms, clean lines, and clear surfaces of twentieth-century design is everywhere evident in this refined and youthful setting that includes Elsa Peretti's cobalt blue pitchers, Tiffany "All Purpose" wineglasses, "Shell and Thread" flatware, and Baccarat "Dyonisos" decanters designed by Tiffany's late Design Director, Van Day Truex.

The "Window" painting is by New York painter Eric Erickson. The metal chairs were designed by Mallet-Stevens in the 1920s.

page 237

*I*n this setting by Modern Bride's editor Cele Lalli for "state of the art" entertaining, there is an informed taste for contemporary electronic age precision, for drama, for sleekness, and for sparkle, all enlivened by touches of Post-Modernist wit.

"Century" flat silver is used with black earthenware plates by Mark Lanzrein, patterned porcelain bowls by Dorothy Hafner, "Shannon" crystal trumpet glasses, and a pair of neo-Palladian pottery candlesticks with surrealist overtones, all from Tiffany's.

Selected Bibliography
· · · · · · · ·

Baldrige, Letitia. *The Amy Vanderbilt Complete Book of Etiquette.* Garden City, N.Y.: Doubleday; revised and expanded, 1978.

Dahl, Stephanie H., and the eds. of *Modern Bride* magazine. *Modern Bride Guide to Your Wedding and Marriage.* New York: Ballantine, 1984.

Follett, Barbara Lee. *Checklist for a Perfect Wedding.* Garden City, N.Y.: Doubleday, 1986.

Gray, Winifred. *You and Your Wedding.* New York: Bantam Books, 1985.

Pritchard, Tom, Billy Jarecki, and Alan Boehmer. *Flowers Rediscovered.* New York: Stewart, Tabori & Chang, 1985.

Mullins, Kathy C., and the eds. of *Bride's Magazine. Bride's Book of Etiquette.* New York: Putnam, 1984.

Piccione, Nancy. *Your Wedding.* Englewood Cliffs, N.J.: Prentice-Hall, 1982.

Post, Elizabeth L. *Emily Post's Complete Book of Wedding Etiquette.* New York: Harper & Row, 1982.

Probert, Christina. *Brides in Vogue since 1910.* New York: Abbeville Press, 1984.

Thomas, Pamela. *Bridal Guide.* La Crosse, Wisconsin: Fifth Avenue Brides Publishing, 1987.

Photography Credits
· · · · · · · ·